M000201066

The Book Of Roasts

The Book Of Roasts

Michael J. Weinstock

THE BOOK OF ROASTS

Copyright © 2017, IT'S A RETIREMENT ACTIVITY, LLC

All rights reserved. No part of this publication may be reproduced, distributed or transmitted in any form or by any means, or stored in a database or retrieval system, without the prior written permission of the copyright holder. For information write to: It's A Retirement Activity, LLC, 17595 Harvard Avenue, #C255, Irvine, CA 92614.

ISBN: 0692873562
ISBN 13: 9780692873564

Dedication

To all the comedians whose ideas inspired me.

Quotes about Roasts

A roast is an event in which a specific individual…is subjected to good-natured jokes at [his] expense intended to amuse the event's wider audience. This type of event was created as a mock counter to a toast. Such events are intended to honor a specific individual in a unique way…The implication is that the *roastee* is able to take the jokes in good humor and not as serious criticism or insult…

- Wikipedia

A roast is an event in which one particular guest is joked about and made fun of by his or her peers…Roasts are traditionally comprised of *insult comedy* and are known to be very vulgar.

- Patrick Bromley, About Entertainment

Insult jokes go back to Abbott and Costello, the Three Stooges, back to people being sort of mean, but in a playful way. The Dean Martin Roasts started doing it as a live forum…We're just taking it further and maybe using a bit more explicit language – and Comedy

Central has been a lot looser on allowing some of that language than they were from the beginning...

- Joel Gallen, Paste

...to criticize severely or ridicule without mercy...an entertainment at which a person...undergoes severe but playful criticism...

- Webster's New World Dictionary

Though the roasting can at times be very mean...[the] goal is to tell jokes that everyone can laugh at - including the *roastee*. "I want the roast to be like a party where everybody goes and has a good time."

- Jeff Ross, NPR

In 2004, psychology professors published a study about the social consequences of disparagement humor, or jokes that belittle or denigrate others...this type of amusement functions as a "social lubricant." This means that roasts, which are a form of disparagement humor, can serve as a way for people to feel more comfortable around each other.

- Health, Attn:

Apology

THIS BOOK IS A SERIES of roasts, so at times it is vulgar, profane, stereotypical, demeaning and irreverent. But it is all in the service of humor. I ask the reader to imagine an event where a friend who knows – and, at heart, loves - the title character is recollecting stories of their shared experiences, with the friend playing a starring role. My intention is not to hurt or offend any individual or group of people. Should the reader find some of the material expressed in this book to be offensive or distasteful, I sincerely apologize in advance, and hope you can find other parts of the book to enjoy.

Contents

Part 1

Lou

WHAT CAN YOU SAY ABOUT Lou? That he is a cathedral of neuroses; that he gives the phrase self-love new meaning; that the size of his shoe is inversely proportional to the size of his pecker; that he is still full of piss and vinegar at 90.

Here's something that defines him: Many years ago while at Hamcke Industries we agreed to go to lunch one day and to meet at his car in the parking lot. He kept me waiting half an hour. When he finally showed up, I angrily asked him if he realized how long I had been waiting. He said, "Of course. I could see you from my office window." I sputtered, "You mean you did that deliberately?" And he said, "I have needs."

I stepped back and considered the man: his monumental insecurity, his three-year confinement at looney-toon central; his preoccupation with flatulence; his utter failure as a salesman, father and husband; his fondness for dwarf-tossing; his claim that God called but he put him on hold; and his cross-dressing conquests on

Hollywood Boulevard. Considering this, I decided his answer was perfectly reasonable.

And did you know you can play Lou like a fine violin? If you want to engage him in passionate, animated conversation, ask him to talk about himself. On the other hand, if you want him to disengage, to tune you out, to look absently around the room, then talk about yourself. I once was able to recite almost the entire poem Jabberwocky before he looked back at me and focused on what I was saying

Finally, you should know that he almost killed me with laughter. We were playing golf at Pebble Beach and approaching a green that had a sand trap on the left, a sand trap on the right, and a cliff overlooking the ocean to the right of that. He hit his approach shot into the left trap. Carefully, he entered the trap, addressed the ball, shuffled his feet in the sand, took a perfectly calculated swing, and lofted the ball over the green and into the right trap. Sitting behind the wheel in the golf cart, I suppressed a giggle.

He then calmly raked the left trap, strode with aplomb across the green, entered the right trap, addressed the ball, shuffled his feet in the sand, took a perfectly calculated swing, and lofted the ball over the green and back into the left trap. By then my forehead was pressed against the steering wheel and my shoulders were convulsing with suppressed laughter.

He then calmly raked the right trap, strode with aplomb across the green, re-entered the left trap, addressed the ball, shuffled his feet in the sand, took a perfectly calculated swing, and lofted the ball over the green, over the right trap, and into the ocean.

At that point I had a choice. I could die of suppressed laughter or I could let loose. They say the fish in the sea and the diners in the clubhouse jumped two feet when my hysterical shriek rolled across the fairways.

Alice

ALICE IS A HORSE OF another color: unkempt, offensive, pony-tailed, mid-fifties. That her view of the world is sardonic goes without saying. She told me she does not hate men; she simply views them as an inconvenience, at best. When confronted with the duplicity of men, she slowly shakes her head from side-to-side and rolls her eyes upward. Some might interpret that as a sign of exasperation. The knowledgeable interpret it as shorthand for, "What an asshole!"

Being cruel, when her first husband who only had hours to live asked her late at night for sex one last time, she exclaimed, "You don't have to get up in the morning!" For spite, she cooked a block of ice when her second husband came home excited from ice fishing. From pique, she mocked her third husband when he accused her of parking too far from the curb by holding her hands three inches apart and saying sweetly, "But you told me this was eight inches." And from pure nastiness, she suggested her fourth husband get a hatbox when he noticed his hair was falling out and asked her what he could use to keep it in.

She believed that after God made men and women and realized they would always fight, he made Mexico. That was her favorite venue for divorce. She would turn her visits into pilgrimages dedicated to the pursuit of high culture such as kitsch, overstuffed bikinis, velvet art, taco cook-offs, under-tipping, over-eating and the seduction of what she liked to refer to as those "swarthy, Latino-types." She also introduced her WASP girlfriend to her Mexican husband, but all they produced was a migrant polo player.

Before her marriages, I noticed she was quite optimistic about meeting men as she scoured the singles bars for guys that were smart, sweet, handsome and career-minded. After a year of searching, she said she would settle for any mammal with a day job. Then, when she had a child and her husband noted that with the baby's tiny arms he would be no weight lifter, and with his tiny legs he would be no long-distance runner, she observed that like his father he would be no porn star.

She took to parenthood easily enough with only a few glitches along the way: like the time she left her baby's carriage in the middle of an intersection while she chased an errant balloon; or the time she tossed him up in the air and into a door frame; or the time she left him in the car for a four-hour facial; or the time she thought she would give him a sister but realized it would interfere with her soaps.

Some say Alice gives womanhood a bad name, but she sees it differently. She sees her activities as offsetting the never-ending propensity of men to act like shmucks. When God said at her birth, "Come forth! Come forth!" she decided to come fifth and has not regretted it since.

Burt

BURT LOVES TO BET ON sports. He lost $50 dollars the last time he tried: $25 on the play and $25 on the instant replay. He is obese, dimwitted, balding, 30, and has an interesting take on athletics. He views all silver medal winners at the Olympics as the first of the worst. He thinks weightlifters who take steroids and testosterone should be classified as Bulgarian women. He believes what was once wrestling in college is now called "date rape." And when his wife complained he never touched her and she wanted to talk about sex, he said, "All right, how often do you think Tom Brady gets laid?"

His athletic skills are unparalleled: He can palm a soft ball; serve with topspin or foreskin; dunk well above five feet; hurl his driver the length of a six-iron; punt sideways; water ski face first; catch the javelin; brush back with the discus; and drop a foul ball without getting mustard on his shirt.

We once went to the beach together. Lying on the blanket, he looked so much like a beached whale they hosed him down. We discussed the unification of general relativity and quantum mechanics;

the collapse of the quantum wave function; whether Dolly Parton had backaches; and where the voice came from that said, "Dig!" He followed all the voice's instructions when it told him to find the chest, take the silver, go to the casino, buy the chips, play Roulette, and bet it all on 16. When the ball landed on 15, the voice said, "Goddamn it"

He also took me flying. After the first touch and go, he lost my luggage. He said it was an economy flight so we only flew over drive-ins. When I failed to eat my sandwich, he complained I was wasting good food and noted there were people starving on Air India. Finally, when we landed he groused that it was a really short runway until I pointed out how wide it was.

Being a generous soul, he likes to have the guys over to watch sports TV. He wears his cap backwards, lets his butt crack show, loops his shorts below his belly, farts with abandon, belches with pride, and swills beer copiously. In short, he is indistinguishable from everyone else in the room. He also serves fried Twinkies, 4,000-calorie burgers, draft beer floats, and chocolate fudge cotton candy. He claims that this kind of Bacchanalia is the only effective antidote men have devised to counteract the officious intermeddling of women.

Finally, he likes to attend the funerals of sports figures. One funeral home he went to was powered by solar panels so it could only roast, not cremate. To a grieving widow who thanked him for coming, he said, "It was my pleasure!" He inadvertently bought a floral arrangement for a famous ballplayer that said, "Good luck in your new location." And when he saw a grinning but dead quarterback arrive at his gravesite propped up behind the wheel of a gold Rolls Royce drawn by four white stallions, he observed, "Man, that's really living!"

Moishe

MOISHE IS A JEWISH RACONTEUR: three-piece suits, baldpate, acerbic, mid-50s. His ruminations are the source of many Jewish jokes. It was he who first observed that Jews do not mind drinking as long as it does not interfere with their suffering. It was he who approached a table of elderly Jewish women at the deli and asked, "Is anything all right?" It was his mother who would not eat for 30 days because she did not want her mouth to be full in case he called. It was he who advised a housewife at wits end that her life would not begin until the last kid left the house and the dog died. And it was he who urged temple ladies to diminish a flasher yanking open his coat by observing, "You call that a lining?" and to mock an obscene caller breathlessly inquiring, "Guess what I have in my hand?" by observing, "Honey, if you've got it in one hand, I'm not interested."

He is also particularly adept at offending the afflicted. On one occasion, an elderly lady from Hadassah was abducted by gorillas while on safari in Africa and ill used by the silverback who had his way with her for six months prior to rescue. She was very depressed when we visited her in the hospital. Moishe held her hand and told her everything would be all right and that time would heal. He comforted her by saying, "I'm sure he'll call, write, send flowers..." On another occasion, he took a blind friend to a Passover Seder, handed him a matzos instead of a prayer book, and chortled when his friend exclaimed, "Who wrote this crap?"

When asked how to improve Christmas, Moishe said, "Put parking meters on the roof."

Moishe is also a scholar. On an oral exam he spelled "cultivate" correctly and was asked to use it in a sentence. He said, "Last vinter on a snowy day, I vas vaiting for a bus. But it was too cultivate, so I took a taxi." He also wrote a book on porn called, "Debbie Does Bupkis." When asked what someone does for fun who is an insomniac, an agnostic and a dyslexic, he said, "Stays up all night wondering if there's a Dog." When questioned where one could get scrod, he congratulated the inquirer for his clever use of the simple past tense and past participle of "screwed." When asked by an anthropologist the difference between a vulture and a Jewish mother, he mused, "At least a vulture waits until you're dead before it eats your heart out." And, when queried by a programmer about what one gets when one combines an Apple and a Jewish American Princess, he replied, "A computer that never goes down."

It was on a road trip that I finally understood his philosophy of life. We came across a one-room schoolhouse in the backcountry and he told me about his education in a similar setting. Trying to influence his thinking, his young teacher asked the class, "Who was the greatest man that ever lived?" Lincoln and Washington were mentioned but the teacher said that was not the answer she was looking for. Finally, Moishe cried out, "Jesus Christ!" and she was thrilled. At recess his friend asked him why he selected Jesus Christ and Moishe replied, "I know Moses was the greatest man that ever lived, but business is business."

Alan

ALAN IS A COMEDIAN: GAUNT, irascible, always broke, pushing 40. We attended a Chinese university in our 20's where he researched how to be funny in Mandarin. He didn't get many laughs but he did receive the kinds of quizzical looks that are easily interpreted in Eastern philosophy as, "What a putz!" After he achieved some success, he was invited back to receive an honorary degree. I am told a horse graduated with an honorary degree from the university after he did. It was the first time in history a college gave an honorary degree to an entire horse.

For a while, Alan tried straight drama. He directed and starred in "The Iceman Cometh." Unfortunately, an inebriated actor he did not get along with said to him on stage, "When the iceman cometh, I hope he cometh all over you." It was then that Alan returned to comedy and went on the road to entertain the troops. He was so popular that when he performed in Afghanistan, they shot at him from both sides. He was also expelled for selling pornographic coloring books to tots.

One reason he may not have achieved more success as a comedian was that his eyes bulged. He could find no doctor who specialized in the problem until he looked up "Eyes Bulging" on the internet. He found a doctor in a seedy part of town, in a run-down building, with an empty waiting room. After consultation, the doctor said, "You have an exceedingly rare condition and for me to cure it I must remove your testicles." Alan left horrified, but later with bulging eyeballs ruining his career and sex life, he finally acquiesced and had the surgery. Indeed, he looked so good he decided to buy a new wardrobe. The tailor he went to was arrogant and declined to measure him because he could see his particulars: he judged a size 42 jacket, a 32-inch inseam, a 36-inch waist and size 40 underwear. Alan demurred, insisting he wore size 34 underwear. The overbearing tailor observed, "You can't wear size 34 underwear because if you did your eyes would bulge out of their sockets!"

Sadly, setbacks in his profession made Alan a regular in local bars where, more often than not, he would drink until he was shit-faced. It just so happened one night that there was a lady at the bar who apparently believed that having to shave her armpits was both sexist and discriminatory. Each time she raised her arm for a drink, the patrons of the bar were riveted by the bush-like display. As the evening wore on, Alan slurred to the bartender, "Hey, I'd like to buy the ballerina a drink." The bartender said, "What makes you think she's a ballerina?" Alan replied, "Any girl who can lift her leg that high, *has* to be a ballerina!"

In the end he became a jaundiced talent scout and that is what finished him off in the business. He auditioned a performer who said he had a very unusual act that he had perfected in Europe and wanted to show it to him. Before Alan could object, the performer jumped on his desk, flapped his arms and flew around the room. Alan said, "So you can imitate birds. What else?"

Karen

KAREN IS A DIVORCE ATTORNEY: tailored, no-nonsense, bitchy, mid-forties. She pacified one irate client by conceding that paying alimony was just like buying oats for a dead horse. She told another that divorce was painful and he could save himself a lot of trouble in the future by finding a woman he hated and buying her a house

Once, I saw her at a fine restaurant having a tremendous argument with her husband after he told her that the beautiful young woman who just entered the restaurant with a girlfriend was his mistress. She sputtered, "That's it, you son-of-a-bitch. I'm filing for divorce." Calmly, he replied, "That's fine. But you can kiss the yacht goodbye as well as the jet, the weekends in Marbella, the Rolls, the getaway in St. Tropez and our Manhattan penthouse." She thought about it for a while, suffering in silence. Then, a friend of her husband's entered the restaurant with another beautiful young woman on his arm and she asked him, "Who's that with Fred?" Her husband replied, "That's his mistress." She thought about it and observed, "Ours is prettier."

Perhaps her most unusual case was the 95-year old man and the 90-year-old woman who went into court for a divorce. The judge looked over the papers and said to Karen, "It seems everything is in order. But, I must ask: They've been married for 70 years. Why have they waited until now to get a divorce?" Karen replied, "They just wanted to wait until the children died."

One year on December 31st, a client called Karen and said he had to see her desperately regarding the split of community property in his divorce. She replied, "George, it's impossible. It's year end and I'm trying to settle three divorce cases that have huge tax implications if they don't get done on time." He pleaded with her, said he only needed five minutes of her time, and promised to pay her $1,000. She thought about it and said, "Okay, come in and sit in the waiting room. If I get a break, I'll come out and see you." It turns out she did get a break about 7 p.m., saw the client, and gave him the advice he needed which made him very happy. He stood up, peeled a $1,000 bill off his roll, and left. After he was gone, Karen looked down at the bill and noticed there was a second $1,000 bill stuck under the first one. Her ethical dilemma? Should she tell her partners?

She also loved telling war stories over cocktails. She told me she once calmed a client by noting that in her practice 50 percent of marriages ended in divorce, but since the other half ended in death, he could be one of the lucky ones. She also received a call from a client who said he wanted to sue for divorce. When she asked him on what grounds, he answered, "Can you believe my wife says I'm a lousy lover." Karen replied "Your being a lousy lover is not grounds for divorce, but her knowing the difference is." Lastly, she encouraged an elderly client who badly wanted a second husband to chat up her new neighbor even though he had been in prison for 30 years for killing his wife and dismembering her body. Karen opined, "He's probably not married?"

Ray

RAY IS A TRAVEL AGENT: smooth, insincere, sycophantic, and 40-ish. He was "comped" on a fancy cruise and brought me along. We toured the ship and he was utterly amazed at the grand scale of shipboard life. A soccer field could have fit inside the grand ballroom. Couches seated 12 or more. The pools accommodated over 300. The banquet tables stretched forever. We dined late one night and, as he got drunk as a skunk, he kept raving about the size of things on the ship. Finally, when his bladder was full, he asked the steward for directions to the men's room, lost his way, and fell into a pool. As he dog-paddled frantically toward the ladder, he screamed, "Don't flush! Don't flush."

It happens that Ray likes to regale his clients with travel stories. He talks about the hijacking of a tourist bus he was on but it was okay because the Japanese tourists got more than 1,500 pictures of the hijackers. He chuckles about the timid tourist who stopped a gruff New York City cop and asked nervously, "Can you tell me how to get to the Empire State Building or should I just go fuck myself?" When he was asked by an airport security officer, "Sir, do you know what's in your luggage?" his replied, "No. I put a bag over my head and packed with my feet. I'm thinking potato chips and dynamite." After being released from custody, he arrived at the plane and accosted the pilot, "If the voice and flight recorders are never damaged during a crash, why isn't the whole damn plane made of that shit?"

Unfortunately, Ray suffered the hazards of the road while checking out some newly built tourist accommodations. He pulled into a hotel late at night exhausted after driving all day and asked the desk clerk for a single room. Waiting for his key, he noticed a lovely blonde in the lobby and went to talk to her. Soon enough, he came back with the blonde on his arm and said to the clerk, "Isn't that a coincidence! Who knew I'd meet my wife here. I guess I'll need a double room for the night." Indeed, the night passed most pleasantly. In the morning, when he went to settle his bill, he was astonished to see he owed more than $3,000. "What the hell is this?" he said to the desk clerk. "I've only been here one night!" "That may be true," said the clerk, "but your wife has been here three weeks."

I once asked him, "Why do they have Bibles in every motel room?" He said, "Beats me. I don't even know why a man would want to read the Bible if he's with a woman. He's already got what he prayed for." And speaking of Bibles, Ray once helped a bishop rent a remote cabin in the mountains so he could slowly and carefully read a photocopy of the original Bible that Ray obtained for him and modified slightly as a practical joke. Several hours after they arrived, Ray went to check up on the bishop. He was bent over the manuscript moaning, weeping, hugging himself, and rocking back and forth. He kept mumbling "No, no, no, oh no…" Feigning alarm, Ray cried out, "Your Eminence, what's wrong?" The bishop pointed to the open page and groaned, "It says celebrate, not celibate."

Oliver

OLIVER IS A RICH SNOB: dapper, bemused, tanned, 52. He can express unbridled contempt just by arching an eyebrow. He loves luxury sports cars. I was with him at his club when a big game hunter noted for tall tales told him about an unusual incident that occurred in the jungle. He heard a lion roaring in distress and when he investigated he saw the lion was trapped in a pit. To his astonishment, a mouse appeared, saw what was happening, ran away, returned with a red Ferrari, tied a rope to the bumper, and pulled the lion out. It was only moments later when the lion was able to return the favor by letting the mouse scramble out of an elephant's footprint by dropping his penis into it. "So, you see," observed the hunter, "with a 12-inch cock, you don't need a red Ferrari." "To the contrary," Oliver countered, "with a red Ferrari, you don't need a 12-inch cock!"

Oliver has firm ideas about finance. He feels a study of the market reveals the best time to buy anything is last year. He points out that among the things money cannot buy is what it used to, and that bills travel through the mail at twice the speed of checks. He knows inflation is bad when he pays cash for something and they ask to see his driver's license, and believes people who say money cannot buy happiness do not know where to shop. Finally, he asserts that money is better than poverty, if only for financial reasons, and that when someone says, "It's not the money, but the principle of the thing," it's the money.

When he gets the chance, he loves to jerk around members of the working class. While strolling in a neighborhood of low-cost housing that he was considering for investment, a little boy apparently swallowed a coin and it got stuck in his throat, so his mother ran out in the street looking for help. Oliver performed the Heimlich maneuver on the boy and the coin popped out. "I don't know how to thank you, doctor…" the mother began. "I'm not a doctor," Oliver replied. "I'm from the IRS."

For a time, Oliver was an investment banker. I was visiting him on Wall Street when a scruffy old man came into his office and said to his secretary, "I wanna to make a fuckin' investment." "Certainly, sir," his secretary replied, "but there's no need to use that kind of language." "Oh, just move it along, lady," the old man growled, "I wanna make a fuckin' investment." "I'll be glad to be of service, sir," she said, blushing slightly, "but I would appreciate not being spoken to in that way." "Jeez, would you let me make a fuckin' investment, already?" he retorted. Flustered and embarrassed, she said she would have to speak with her boss and went to get Oliver. When Oliver arrived, he asked how he could be of service. "I just won the $40 million lottery," the old man said, "and I wanna make a fuckin' investment." "I see," said Oliver, "and this bitch is giving you trouble?"

Oliver ended his business career on a down note when, as president of a commercial bank, he ordered his tellers to place a sign above their stations saying, "To err is human, to forgive is not bank policy." He was on the street by noon.

Butch

BUTCH IS A STEELWORKER: HANDSOME but crude, tough but sentimental, clever but saucy, and cynical beyond his 37 years. He loves to tease, say silly things, play practical jokes, and make wry comments in rapid succession.

He claims he spends a lot of time studying insects and has concluded, "Ant farms are good, though it's hard to find harvesters that small. Centipedes are good, though it takes time to put on their shoes. Killer bees are good, but only to plot murder." And finally, "Ants, who can carry many times their weight, should carry beer nuts."

He grew up in a world of blast furnaces, cast iron, carbon reduction, and bars and ingots: all changing with technology. He loved to jerk supervisors around whenever he could get away with it. One day he was put at the controls of a machine that was supposed to extrude ingots at a high rate per hour, but pretended he could not get it to work so he asked the foreman for help. The foreman came over, inspected the machine, made sure everything was in working order, and pushed the starter button causing the engine to roar into life. Butch jumped and exclaimed, "What's the hell was that?"

I did everything I could to heighten his cultural awareness, to show him the finer things in life. But he would mock me. We would stroll through botanical gardens and each time we passed a lovely arrangement of flowers he would sigh and say "Wow!" When I asked why, he said, "I can't believe so many funerals take place in such a small space at the same time." When I asked him if he believed in reincarnation he said "No, and I didn't believe in it the first time around." And when I asked him if he thought Astrology was real, he said, "As a Sagittarius, I would say no."

At the ballet, he observed, "Everyone should be taller rather than running around on tiptoes." At the art museum, he muttered, "They should have hung the painter." At the opera, he opined, "Singing in a foreign language is about as dumb as calling a football game in German." And at a truly awful symphony, when the man sitting next to him started to weep, I asked him, "Is he sad?" and Butch said, "No, he's a composer."

Butch drank too much and remembered too little. We would bar-hop late into the night, and I never enjoyed my conversations with him more than when he tried to slur his way into intelligibility. Sometimes, sadly, he would throw up on himself. This was no problem for me but it played havoc with his sweet but understanding girlfriend, Connie, with whom he shared an apartment. She was the only person he was afraid of; so one time when he arrived home very late he told her someone else had thrown up on him. She accepted that without comment. The next day, to maintain his credibility, he called her from the jobsite and said he found the guy who threw up on him and gave him a slap upside the head. Connie said, "You might as well hit him again. He crapped in your jockey's, too!"

Sadie

YOU WILL RECALL THE LAST time we heard about Sadie, she was entering the nursing home at 80, and although she is now 85, stooped, wizened and grizzled, she is as much a pisser as ever.

My uncle, who also stays at the home, told me about her recent antics. Apparently, most folks consider her top-tier obnoxious because of her haughty attitude, her in-your-face confrontational style, and her incessant bragging. She brags about her travels, her dead husbands, her kids and grandkids, her famous friends, and her wealth. But what really gets my uncle's goat is her repeated insistence she can tell everything about a person just by looking at him. My uncle thinks that is ridiculous and tells her so every chance he gets. One time, just to show her up, he said to her, "I bet you can't guess my age." She shot back, "The hell I can't! Unzip your fly." Not wanting to back down, he did so. Without hesitation, she reached into his pants and starting massaging his genitals for five minutes, ten minutes, then fifteen minutes. Finally, she spat out, "You're 87." Stunned, he said, 'My God, how did you know?" She smiled sweetly, "You told me yesterday."

I heard she even dissed a frail codger. He told her he had gotten incredibly lucky and had sex with a liberated 25-year-old who showed him a great time. The trouble was, he had developed a discharge and did not know what to do about it. Sadie asked him, "Do you remember her name?" He said he did. She asked, "Do you remember where she lives?" He said he thought so. She asked, "Do you remember her exact address?" He said yes. She asked, " Will she still be friendly toward you?" He said of course. So, she advised him, "Hurry back. You're coming."

My uncle also tells a story about Sadie that is hard to credit. It seems three other residents of the nursing home were rocking back and forth on the front porch. Mrs. Green was on the right, Mrs. Black was on the left, and Mr. Smith was in the middle. After awhile, Mrs. Green leaned over and said to Mr. Smith, "Do you mind if I hold your penis?" He smiled, thanked her for her generosity, and noted that if he needed his penis held, he would ask Mrs. Black to do it. Mrs. Green was quite put out by that and later complained to Sadie, "That's really unfair. How come Mrs. Black gets to hold Mr. Smith's penis and not me?" Sadie replied dryly, "Because she's got palsy."

Another time, Sadie advised a codger who just arrived at the nursing home that whatever he did he must not lean to the right and he must not lean to the left because if he did, a staffer would rush over and straighten him up. He asked, "To keep me from falling over?" "No," she said. "passing gas is prohibited."

Lastly, she loves to feign memory loss. When a resident introduced her to one of his daughters, she said, "I can't remember. Did you die or was it your sister?"

Part 2

Jackson

OF COURSE WE WOULD CALL Jackson a hunter, though his appearance belies that assertion. It is hard to imagine any animal being fearful when confronted with a rotund, hirsute, besotted, 28-year-old, swearing and crashing through the bush.

They say he was arrested for killing and eating a bald eagle. They hauled him before a judge who asked, "How could you do that? How could you kill and eat an animal that is the symbol of our country; the symbol of freedom? How could you so cavalierly destroy an endangered species?" Without showing contrition, Jackson replied, "Your honor, I was lost in the woods for five days and was starving to death. I got lucky and snared the eagle and had to eat it to survive." The judge considered that and ruled in Jackson's favor. But he was curious so he asked, "Tell me, what does a bald eagle taste like?" Jackson shrugged and said, "Pretty much like a spotted owl."

We had a spirited discussion about the fairness of humans killing innocent animals. He defended it on the grounds that many of them are just plain vicious. He cited the ti-lion that he pursued in the jungles of Borneo and was as nasty and snarling as can be imagined. I asked, "What makes him so mean?" "He said, "He has a lion's head on one end and a tiger's head on the other." I said, "That's ridiculous. If he has a head on both ends, he can't crap." Examining his fingernails, Jackson sighed, "That's why he's so mean."

Jackson also opined that it is not bestiality if done with an animal of the same faith.

Once, when he badly needed money and was high on ecstasy, he answered an ad placed by the zoo for a surrogate to mate with a fierce female gorilla that had frightened all the other males in the enclosure. When he saw his intended, he insisted that her arms and legs be chained and that a bag be placed over her head. As he plied his trade, her arms came loose and wrapped around his neck. Then, her legs came loose and wrapped around his body. Finally, he started screaming, "Get it off! Get it off!" The zookeeper yelled, "What, her arms or her legs?" "No," Jackson bellowed, "the bag, man, I wanna kiss her!"

His favorite story relates to the time he lived on a farm to learn about animal physiology and was put in charge when the farmer was away, Late one night, there was a knock on the door and a Muslim, Hindu and lawyer appeared saying their car had broken down and asking if he could he put them up for the night. He said, "Sure, but we only have two guest beds so one of you will have to sleep in the barn." The Hindu volunteered. After a while, there was a knock on the door. It was the Hindu and he said, "There's a cow in the barn. I can't sleep there." The Muslim and Hindu agreed to switch places. Shortly thereafter, there was a knock on the door. It was the Muslim and he said, "There is a pig in the barn. I can't sleep there." The Muslim and lawyer agreed to switch places. Shortly thereafter, there was a knock on the door. It was the cow and the pig…

Bobby

IT IS HARD TO ROAST a child of four but it can be done, probably poorly. But Bobby is so sweet and innocent, so well intentioned, so eager to please, that he can hardly be spared the vitriol.

I overheard him having a long discussion with his twin sister about where babies come from. They speculated on various stork theories, possible gifts from Santa, the contributions of the Easter Bunny, and the leavings of the Tooth Fairy. At one point his sister said, "Remember the picture we saw in Dad's magazine where the man put his pee pee in the woman's mouth. Maybe that's where babies come from." Bobby replied, "No, I showed the picture to Mom and asked if that was where baby's came from?" She said, "No, sweetheart, that's where jewelry comes from."

Another time we were in Bobby's garage, checking the oil in his dad's car, when he blurted out, "What's a penis?" I was so startled I was not sure what to say, so I advised him to ask his mother. He barged into the kitchen and through the open window I could hear him ask her, "Hey, Mom, what's a penis?" Taken aback, she advised him to ask his father who was taking a shower upstairs. He stomped up the stairs and again, through an open window, I could hear him say, "Hey, Dad, what's a penis?" His Dad replied, "You want to know what it is. I'll show you." I thought I heard the rustle of a towel being removed and his Dad said, "*That* is a penis! And not only that, that is a *perfect* penis!" I heard, "Thanks, Dad!" followed by feet pounding down the stairs and soon enough Bobby was back in the garage. Out of breath, he exclaimed, "I know what it is!" I said, "Show me." He dropped his pants and underpants, pointed to himself and declared, "*That* is a penis! And if it were two inches shorter, it would be a *perfect* penis!"

Even though it was early in their lives, Bobby's pre-school teacher tried to get the kids in his class to understand the difference between making deposits in the bank and getting receipts from the bank. She asked Bobby, "When your Dad deposits money in the bank, what does he get back?" Bobby piped up, "A toaster!"

Bobby also had trouble understanding why his mother made such a fuss about him still sucking his thumb after he stumbled into her bedroom without knocking one night and saw her sucking something that looked just like it, only bigger.

Finally, being Jewish, Bobby was taken to his first bris shortly after his fourth birthday. He was fascinated by the whole procedure: particularly when the mohel put the excised foreskin in his pocket. He had a lot of questions for the mohel and then told his sister what he had learned. He said, "That man over there told me he keeps the skins he gets and makes wallets out of them and sells them for a lot of money." His sister asked, "Why a lot of money?" Bobby answered, "He says when you rub them, they turn into something called *attaché cases.*"

Arnold

ARNOLD DID NOT ACHIEVE REAL recognition as a leading biologist until, at 40, he published his seminal paper, "The Secret Life Of Wombats." In demeanor, he was the living embodiment of the absent-minded professor. In speech, he talked in bursts.

To his credit he would go to any length, endure any inconvenience, and suffer any embarrassment in pursuit of his research on animals. It was that dedication and commitment that took him to a bar late one night where his friend said they were selling unique frogs for high prices. Sure enough, behind the bar sat a normal looking frog with a sign next to it that said "Frog for sale. $1,500." He asked the bartender why the frog cost so much and the bartender said, "That frog gives the best blow job on the planet." Arnold ignored the sexual boast but bought the frog for research purposes only on condition he could return it and get his money back if his research proved fruitless. Three weeks later, his wife got back from a business trip and found Arnold stark naked in the kitchen holding the frog in one hand and a cookbook in the other. Surrounding him were bubbling pots, sizzling frying pans, grinding knife sharpeners, and churning mixers. She said, "What the hell is going on here?" He answered, "Honey, if I can teach this frog to cook, you're outta here."

Arnold also conducted extensive research on chimps and there were two, a male and a female, that he grew quite fond of. When they were old and infirm he found them a home with a nice, elderly lady. She loved them as he did, and when they died she said she would miss them terribly and asked Arnold if he thought it would be a good idea to have them mounted. He advised, "It would probably be better if they just hold hands."

I was actually with Arnold when he uploaded his notes to a Washington, D.C., database as part of a nationwide experiment on species cross breeding. He was given the assignment of mating a male mouse with a female giraffe. The mouse passed away and Arnold's notes were succinct in his description of the cause. He wrote, "Between the kissing and the fucking and the kissing and the fucking, the mouse must have run 500 miles."

Arnold was also a consultant to a biologist trying to mate a man and a goat. The experiment was exceptionally difficult to arrange. First, it was very hard to find a human willing to participate, but the promise of lots of money finally produced a farm boy conversant with the ways of the barnyard. Second, a certain totally unanticipated action occurred during the mating. Third, although the mating itself was easy enough to accomplish, the results were very difficult to interpret in a meaningful way because the unanticipated action was beyond the scope of the experiment. The biologist was baffled and after consulting various textbooks without success, he turned to Arnold and told him, "They mated successfully just as the experiment required, but when they were done, to my surprise the goat turned around and licked him off." Arnold observed, " A good goat will do that."

Barry

GULLIBLE IS AS GULLIBLE DOES. Is Barry easily cheated or tricked? Definitely. Is he credulous? Certainly. Is he deceivable? No doubt. How about foolable? Check. Deludable? Check. Exploitable, hoodwinkable, victimizable? Check, check, check. In other words, an all-around nice guy a dollar short and a day late; a 25-year old Adonis with looks, not brains.

His first job was as an assistant to a cinematographer. He manned the back-up camera for a gigantic bridge collapse in an action movie. The company had received permission from a corrupt government in the tropics to blow up the bridge, which was slated for demolition anyway. The bribe took a third of the film's budget. Getting the one-time shot was crucial so the director used five different cameras, the back-up one being assigned to Barry who had the least experience. The scene commenced, the charges were fired, and the bridge collapsed span by span into a cataclysmic fireball of dust and debris. Because of the topical heat and humidity and the unreliability of the power supply, the first four cameras reported in one by one that they had missed the shot. In desperation the director shouted to Barry up in his perch, "Barry, did you get the shot?" Barry yelled back, "Whenever you're ready!"

Barry loved America. He observed, "Where else could you be down on your luck and be picked up by a Good Samaritan and taken to his home and offered new clothes and a hot bath and a fine meal and a warm bed and a sumptuous breakfast." I asked, "This happened to you?" He answered, "No, to my sister."

Barry remembers the time he lost his innocence in a sex motel that offered half hour rates, porn on TV, and mirrors on the ceiling. I asked him, "Was she pretty?" He replied, "No, I was alone."

Just last month I was playing golf with Barry and his foxy girlfriend in Ireland when he hit the hell out of a drive and watched in horror as the ball came down in the middle of the foursome ahead of us and knocked a golfer flat. When we arrived, the golfer was fine and when asked how he survived such a blow he said, "I'm a leprechaun. And because you've been so solicitous, I will grant you three wishes to my one." Barry made three wishes and the leprechaun confirmed (1) there was a check for $1,000,000 waiting for him in his hotel room, (2) plus airline tickets, (3) plus passes to the great golf courses of the world. Then, the leprechaun said, "For my wish, I want to have sex with your girlfriend." Barry was irate and about to slug the leprechaun when his girlfriend pulled him aside and said, "What's the matter with you? Don't you realize that for a half hour of meaningless sex we can be on easy street for the rest of our lives?" Barry groused and argued but she assured him she loved him and that this would not change anything between them. Finally, he relented and the leprechaun went into the woods with her and had his way. On their walk back, I heard him ask, "How old is your boyfriend?" She said "25." And he said, "Imagine that, 25 years old and he still believes in leprechauns."

Dustin

You have to admit, as golf pros go, Dustin is everyone's dream walking: dirty blonde hair, slender, tan, white teeth, plaid pants, only the best golf shirts. He would have been the youngest golfer to ever play on the pro tour but that did not work out so well, so at 35 he became club pro at Westchester's toniest country club.

As a good friend, he was always generous with his time and often gave me lessons for free at the club's driving range. He had just finished helping me with my backswing and release when a beautiful club member came over and asked him to help her with her swing. She was a mess: hooking slicing, topping, chunking. After watching her for a while, he stopped her and said, " I think I can help. Your swing is fine but your problem is with your grip. Now, I'm going to make a suggestion and please don't take offense, but I think it would help if you held the club the same way you would hold your husband's penis." Naturally she blushed but went back up on the tee and stared hitting screaming drives dead center down the range, one after another. Finally, he stopped her and said, "That's great. You're a quick learner. But I would like you to do one thing differently. Go back up on the tee, take the club out of your mouth, and hold it in your hands like this…"

After failing to make the pro tour, Dustin tried medical school for a while and took a class on involuntary contractions. The professor was getting frustrated trying to get the concept of involuntary contractions across to a pretty young wife sitting next to Dustin who just did not get it no matter how many examples the professor gave. To help her, Dustin leaned over and whispered, "What is your asshole doing when you have an orgasm?" She whispered back, "Probably playing golf with his friends."

From time to time Dustin would let down his hair over drinks and tell me about some of the odd things that happened to him on the course. He played an entire round one-day with a very rich member who wanted more sustained instruction than what he could get in just a few lessons. They were on the 8th hole when the member hit a huge slice off the tee with the ball landing behind a barn. The member was about to chip back onto the fairway when Dustin said, "Wait a minute. I've a better idea. Let me open the barn doors on both sides and you can hit a 3-iron through the barn and be on in two." The member said, "No, no. The last time I tried that something terrible happened. I was playing with my wife and she suggested the same thing, but I hit a beam trying to get through the barn and the ball ricocheted around and hit her in the temple." Shocked, Dustin said, "How awful! What happened?" The member sighed, "I took a seven."

He also told me that, contrary to popular belief, a golf pro's life could be quite hazardous. A fellow pro was having an affair with a club member's wife when her husband called home while he was having sex with her. The butler told the husband he could see them going at it through the atrium. The irate husband demanded the butler get his rifle and shoot her in the head and him in the balls. He got them with one shot.

Tyler

WHEN TYLER RIDES IN OFF the range neither the pinto pony, the weathered face, the spurs, the chaps, or the cowboy hat slung low seem out of place. Though he looks 50, he is in his thirties, and has a lifetime of hard times and hard wrangling behind him.

He told me about the time he rode into a small town in Northern Colorado after being in the saddle for six months and wrangling a herd down from its winter range. He noticed two things when he rode in: a sheep corral at the beginning of town and the complete absence of women, but thought no more about it. His first act was to buy two bottles of whiskey in the hotel's saloon, take them to his room, drink them in the bath, and sleep for a week. After that, he ate a fine meal and asked the bartender where he could find a woman. The bartender said, "We don't have any women here. But if you're horny, you can always lasso a cute sheep in the corral." Tyler was disgusted and declined. As the weeks wore on, he kept asking about women, the bartender kept talking about sheep, Tyler said he knew he was being set up for ridicule, and the bartender assured him it was not so. Finally, he relented, lassoed a fetching ewe, and all hell broke loose when he walked it through the saloon with howling cowboys jumping out of windows, hiding behind the bar, and rushing out the swinging doors. He barked at the bartender, "You bastard! You told me no one would make fun of me!" The bartender shot back, "It's not that. You got Johnny Ringo's girl!"

Another time, Tyler broke his leg when he was deep in the backcountry and was thrown from his horse after a rattler spooked it. Having great confidence in the horse, he ordered it through clenched teeth to go get help. The horse galloped away and a half-hour later galloped back dropping a beautiful naked blonde onto Tyler's lap. Frustrated, Tyler whistled the horse over and when it lowered its head, he hissed to it, "Watch my lips. Bring *posse!*"

Some of Tyler's co-wranglers were not too swift and Tyler was quick to pounce. One time he and a friend were walking past a corral and came upon a dog licking its balls. His friend said wistfully, "I wish I could do that," and Tyler advised, "You may want to scratch his belly first."

Tyler told me about his friend, Beth, who grew up in a small southern town with her twin sister, Rose. Their mother wanted them to meet new people so when they got to college age she sent Rose to the local Baptist College and Beth to Berkeley. When Christmas vacation rolled around, the girls got to talking and Rose complained her college was too strict and boring. Beth said, "Not mine. Berkeley is a strange place. They have men there who make love to other men, and women there who make love to other women." Rose said, " Yuck, what do they call them?" Beth responded, "They call them 'homos' and 'dikes,' and not only that, they have men there who kiss women on their private parts." Rose gasped, "Yuck, what do they call them?" Sighing, Beth confided, "Well, when I caught my breath, I called him 'precious!'"

Dean

DEAN IS ONE OF THE sleaziest talent agents in Hollywood, bar none. In 20 years, he has seen it all. He can wangle any client into a "D" movie, outdrink them during happy hour, recommend offering sex for bit parts, swap producer credits for cash, and sign contracts without consent. His cigars, comb over, beer belly, and wiseacre attitude provoke fear in some actors and hives in others. They say if you want to be truly forgotten in Hollywood, hire Dean as your agent.

Dean has two major problems: he is enamored with booze and scared shitless of his wife's harangues when he comes home the worse for wear. He therefore does everything he can to not wake her when he staggers home in the wee hours, removes his shoes, tiptoes up the stairs, takes a whiz, and tries to slip into bed unnoticed. Unfortunately, on one occasion when he was in his cups, he tripped over a curb and crushed a bottle of bourbon he was carrying in front of his belly. It bled profusely. When he got home, he put as many bandages on the cuts as he could and slipped into bed confident he had again made it home safely. The next morning at breakfast his wife barked, "You were drunk again last night, weren't you, you son of a bitch?" Feigning innocence, he asked, "What makes you say that?" She said, "There were Band-Aids all over the bathroom mirror!"

He once said to me in a bar, "You've been drinking, haven't you?" I replied, "Why do you ask that?" He said, "You look fuzzy as hell!"

Dean also brags about his many contacts. I decided to call his bluff once and bet him $1,000 he would know no one in Denver. When we arrived at the airport, he had six friends waiting for him, so I doubled the bet for Pittsburgh. And it only got worse. We went from city to city, here and abroad, with bigger and bigger welcoming crowds, increasing the bet until I owed him more than I could possibly afford. Taking pity, he said, "I'll tell you what. Not only will I know people in Moscow, I'll get an audience with Putin." I accepted the bet willingly. He went into the Kremlin and as I waited for him in Red Square it filled up with about 100,000 people. Suddenly, they let out a huge roar when Putin came out on the balcony of Lenin's tomb with Dean right behind him. I groaned, bankrupt. A little kid started yanking on my coat and when I asked him what he wanted, he looked up at the tomb and said, "Who's the Commie with Dean?"

He also told me that the reason divorces in Hollywood are so expensive is because they are worth it, and that therapists set aside zero parking spaces for their narcissistic clients because otherwise there would be no place to park.

His favorite dream is where a fairy godmother tells him he can have any wish he wants but his ex-wife, whom he loathes, will get double. He thinks about money, fast cars, expensive yachts, villas abroad, and even good health, but in the end he asks to be beaten half to death.

Elena

ELENA IS NURSE RATCHET PERSONIFIED, but colder, more heartless, more tyrannical and a battle-axe to the core. In her 50 years, she has never once comforted a patient successfully. You might say her manner is more curbside than bedside; her personal touch more icy than warm.

As a younger woman, she told me about a train trip she took to Philadelphia to present a paper on structural differences in male genitalia by ethnic group. She was part of a larger study on sexual practices in America sponsored in part by her nursing school. A fairly good-looking guy sat down next to her on the train and proceeded to do the New York Times crossword puzzle in record time, his hands flying over the page. His obvious intelligence impressed her, so she was receptive when he struck up a conversation. They talked about her paper and he asked about her findings. She said, "Strangely enough, we found that American Indians have the thickest penises, and Jewish men have the longest." Their conversation was still going strong when the train pulled into the station and she asked his name. He smiled and said, "Tonto Schwartz." Not one to be easily amused, she put him in the schmuck category when she discovered the crossword puzzle he completed was a day old.

She also told me about her favorite medical fantasy where she is assisting with a patient who feels awful even though there seems to be nothing wrong with her. In response to a series of questions, the patient tells the doctor she eats healthy, exercises every day, makes love to her adoring husband every night at 9:15, and loves her job. The doctor opines it is a bacterial infection and prescribes an antibiotic for her. In her fantasy, Elena then eavesdrops on a conversation among three bacteria in the patient's body as to how they are going to escape the antibiotic. One says he is going to hide behind the ear. The second says he is going to hide under the big toenail. The third says, "Look, you guys do what you want to, but I'm riding out of here on the 9:15."

Elena said I reminded her of a young patient she was nicer to than she should have been. He was sick and fading fast and pleaded with her for one last blowjob before he died. She, of course, refused in a huff. But he was persistent and resolute and this impressed her even more than the deterioration of his health. Finally, because it was an indifferent act for her, she relented. After she was finished the patient's phone rang and he said, "Aren't you going to get that, you cocksucker?"

She married a patient and found out during her honeymoon that it might have been a huge mistake. She and her new husband approached the reception desk of a luxury hotel and her husband asked the desk clerk, "We just got married. Would you have something special for us?" The clerk said, "How about the bridal?" The husband thought about it and said, "No, I'll just hold her by the ears until she gets it right."

To Elena, the difference between syphilis and a condo is that you can get rid of syphilis.

Mike

MIKE IS NOT JUST A fireman; he is a great fireman. No woman would mind being rescued by such a big, strong, silent, rugged, blue-eyed hunk. He had it all and had seen it all by 35, sometimes with his tongue firmly in his cheek.

He was called to assist in a home emergency in a fairly wealthy neighborhood. Apparently, a homeowner's wife had managed to get herself stuck in the toilet seat in her master bath and was hysterical not only because she was stuck but because she was naked. She must have pleaded with her husband for something to cover her privates because when Mike arrived there was a cowboy hat over her genitals and an arm over her breasts. Mike examined the toilet carefully and then, with a look of concern on his face, said to the husband, "Well, I've got good news for you and bad news for you. The good news is that we can get your wife out of there. The bad news is the cowboy's a goner."

It goes without saying that Mike is proud of his endowments. We were on a flight together one winter and a very pretty woman sat down between us in coach. When he crossed his leg, she noticed his shoe was huge and asked how he measured it? He confessed he went to a special clothing and shoe store for large men and they had a sizing device that accommodated his foot. Later, when dinner was served and he removed his gloves, she noticed they were unusually large and asked how he measured them? He said he bought his gloves at the same store as his shoes and they had different size samples for customers to try. Finally, after several drinks, she slurred, "Please don't take offense, but I must ask: How long is your penis?" He smiled, "Two inches." Stunned, she asked, "How do you measure it?" He smiled, "From the floor."

During his down time at the firehouse, Mike became an equal opportunity disparager. He opined, "God created women because sheep don't do windows, and created men because vibrators don't paint houses."

He also spent some time in the hospital after being badly injured fighting a 5-alarm fire. His entire body was in a cast and bandages covered his face. The only way they could feed him intravenously was through his rectum. During his stay in the hospital, a sympathetic nurse offered to ease his suffering by giving him some frozen yogurt through his feeding tube. When she was finished and started to leave the room, Mike cried out, "Please come back! Please come back!" She rushed to his side and asked, "Are you in pain? Was it too chilly?" He said, "No, I hate strawberry!"

Mike was driving with a friend from abroad when a fire truck blazed by with sirens howling and a Dalmatian dog sitting on the front seat. His friend asked, "Do they use the dog for crowd control?" Mike said "Actually, no." His friend said, "Well, is he some kind of good luck charm?" Mike said, "Not really." Puzzled, his friend said, "Well, why is he on the truck?" Mike replied, "To help locate fire hydrants."

Iggy

MUSSORGSKY'S "PICTURES AT AN EXHIBITION" was a beautiful piano suite representing a visitor taking a walking tour of paintings at an art exhibition. Similarly, my day with Iggy at the Senior Home for Retired Musicians was a sitting tour of the pictures in his photo album memorializing his raucous life as a jazz trombonist: a life filled with booze and broads, jazz and jail, drugs and dames, and sarcasm and salaciousness.

His first photo showed him chopping into ice with a pick and shovel. He said he wanted to go ice fishing even though drunk, and a perfect stranger kept coming over to him and telling him there were no fish there. He relocated three times and finally said to the stranger, "Who are you, the game warden?" The stranger said, "No, the goalie."

His next photo showed him standing in front of a bank holding his trombone in one hand and a CD in the other. He took the photo to impress a lady who often observed, "Unlike a musician, a CD matures and makes money."

His next photo showed him seated at a bar with six shot glasses arrayed in front of him. He said they were magic and could change a dog into a fox.

His next photo showed him arm in arm with a beautiful young man in front of a bandstand. It was taken during his "sexual adventure" days. He said his lover was exceptionally hairy and claimed it was due to his regularly applying Vaseline all over. Iggy doubted it because, if it were true, his asshole would have grown a ponytail.

His next photo showed a large chicken sitting at a bar. It was actually Iggy stopping in for a quick one on his way home from a costume party. He asked for a scotch and soda and gave the bartender a twenty, but only got five dollars in change. After a while, the bartender sidled up to him and observed that not too many chickens came in for a drink. Iggy said, "I'm not surprised, considering the prices."

His next photo showed him sitting on the floor of a cocktail lounge in Casper, Wyoming, after a cowboy knocked him on his ass. He said he was watching TV at the bar when Donald Trump came on the screen and Iggy said that there was a true horse's ass. The cowboy, who was sitting next to him, belted him and after he shook himself off and got back up on his stool, Iggy observed out loud that Casper must be Trump country. The bartender said, "No, it's actually horse country."

His next photo, taken from the rear of a stage, showed Iggy playing in a pickup band backing Pat Boone at a concert in Des Moines. He said it was the only concert he ever played where the front row had 60 legs and seven teeth.

The final photo showed Iggy wearing a blue burnoose, holding a gold scimitar, and riding a pink pig. He said he was Lawrence of Poland.

Part 3

Deshawn

DeShawn is the biggest, sweetest, kindest, blackest NFL tackle I ever met. Only eight years out of college, his career is nothing but trophies, All-Star games, playoff championships, and a Super Bowl. He would not hurt a fly but loves projecting a fierce demeanor and wounding with a quip. He has a lovely wife and three adorable children.

We had just finished dinner at a nice restaurant and were draining our alligators in the men's room when a skinny kid stepped up next to DeShawn at the urinal and could not resist checking out his equipment. Suddenly, he exclaimed, "My God! I don't believe it! You have a W and Y tattooed on your penis just like me. My wife and I were having marital trouble and I asked her what I could do to prove my love and she said I should tattoo her name on my penis. When I'm soft, it says 'WY' just like you. But when I'm hard, it says 'Wendy.' What does yours say when it's hard?" DeShawn gave him a big smile and said, "Welcome to Jamaica. Have a nice day."

DeShawn loves to swim lap after lap in an Olympic-sized pool to stay in shape. One morning he was swimming his laps when an obnoxious long-distance swimmer kept asking when he would be finished with the lane. It got to a point where DeShawn was so irritated he muttered, "When I finish pissing."

He also swears the best resistance training he gets is in the master bedroom.

He once played in a critical game with a quarterback who was a little slow on the uptake and had a great deal of trouble improvising once the ball was snapped. Just as a play was about to start a crazed mother rushed onto the field and dumped her baby in the quarterback's arms. He threw it for a touchdown.

In another game, DeShawn lined up again and again opposite a defensive end that had been hit in the head one too many times. The end was so focused on destroying whoever lined up against him, he kept mumbling each time he assumed a 3-point stance, "I'm gonna kill Keyshaw Jones! I'm gonna kill Keyshaw Jones!" DeShawn pointed out, "You're Keyshaw Jones."

DeShawn would often take responsibility for something he did not do. Usually, it was because someone pissed him off, or bullied a person who could not fight back, or was just too obnoxious for his taste. One year there was a sportswriter in the locker room that nobody could stand. He was really only interested in scandal and put-downs and inducing one player to criticize another. On top of that he was a braggart. If it was not about his sexual conquests, it was about his hot sports car. One day, he came steaming into the locker room demanding to know who had painted tits on his car. DeShawn slowly unwound himself from his stool, rising ever higher until he stood like a six-and-a-half-foot scarred, ripped, monolith, and said, "I did." The sportswriter hesitated a moment and said, "In case you wanted to know, the first coat is dry."

Hannah

JUST LOOKING AT HER YOU would think Hannah is everyone's sweet aunt or a portly but compassionate high school principal or a smiling server at the neighborhood soup kitchen, but in fact she is the leading sex therapist in Beverly Hills and she slices, dices and vivisects with the best of them. Indeed, her professional opinion is that deflating egos enhances sexual performance.

When she was in medical school she was having trouble deciding which specialty to pursue. She also married young and though her husband was sexually experienced, she was quite naive. They had been married only a year or so and were having difficulty in bed, so her husband suggested they see a sex therapist and she reluctantly agreed. The therapist posed a battery of questions about their sex life and finally asked, "Do you have mutual climax?" Hannah thought about it and said, "No, I think we have State Farm." After that, and after she dumped her husband, her problems in bed cleared up and she knew she had found her calling.

Unfortunately, her sexual problems reasserted themselves some years later when her second husband found his staff softening.

Their teenage son was a whiz in chemistry and developed a liquid formula that could stiffen objects immersed in it. Her husband took heart and said to the son, "Let me borrow your formula, and if it works for me I'll buy you a Chevy." I asked Hannah if her son ever got the Chevy?" She answered, "Yes, he keeps the Chevy in the carport and the BMW I bought him in the garage."

Because her work brought her into contact with so many interesting men, Hannah succumbed to several affairs. She remained one fool's mistress for several years; he was a fool because of his never-ending demands for oral sex even though she advised him that variety was the spice of life. Finally, he died and Hannah took his ashes to a cesspool under construction and said, "Harry, here's the blow job you always asked for," and she blew his ashes into the pit.

For a while, Hannah owned a sex shop so she could research sex toys. I asked her what the best sellers were? She said, "Dildos, without question. Three days ago I sold a white woman a black dildo for $20. Two days ago I sold a black woman a white dildo for $30. And yesterday I sold a Polish woman a plaid dildo for $200." I asked, "Why was the plaid dildo so expensive?" She said, "It was my thermos."

Hannah defines "safe sex" as having thick carpeting so you do not rug-burn your knees.

During one of her research projects, she played the role of a receptionist at a sperm bank. A patient with private insurance came in for an "extraction" which was performed with great skill by a beautiful young nurse. As he returned to the waiting room, he found it filled with half a dozen men masturbating to sex magazines. He said to Hannah, "Who are those guys?" She replied, "They're with HMOs."

Maynard

MAYNARD REALIZED HIS LIFE LONG dream when he became an astronaut. He paid his dues as a top jet pilot, wing commander and general's aide, and now rides thundering rockets into space. He is clear-eyed, smooth-skinned, sun-tanned, and V-shaped, and few can resist his easy manner, wit and charm. At 40, he is a lady-killer.

Al Qaeda in Iraq briefly captured him when he had a flame out during a combat mission. He was lucky to escape. I asked, "What was it like?" and he said, "Well, I learned one thing for sure. The difference between a terrorist and a woman with PMS is you can negotiate with the terrorist."

Sex in space was forbidden. But with high hopes Maynard went into a PX to buy some condoms and had to confess to the saucy counter girl he did not know his size. She told him to measure himself using the three holes in the wall at the back of the men's dressing room. He tried two and when he pushed into the third a pair of exquisite lips wrapped around his member and made his eyeballs roll up in his head. Back at the counter the girl asked with a knowing smile,

"Do you know what size condom you want?" He said, "The hell with the condoms. I want to buy the wall!"

Maynard was once the navigator on a shuttle flight to the space station. They were trying to catch up to the station at 18,000 miles per hour when the aircraft's orbital dynamics system went out. The commander asked Maynard for a status update and Maynard replied, "I'm afraid we're lost, but we're making great time."

I actually attended a preflight briefing that Maynard, as flight commander, was giving to an international crew of astronauts. While he was reading his notes, someone sneezed and he asked angrily, "Who sneezed?" No one answered so he ordered the Russian off the flight. He asked again, "Who sneezed?" No one answered so he ordered the Japanese off the flight. He asked again, "Who sneezed?" A Brit quietly replied, "I did." Maynard said, "Bless you."

On another spaceflight, Maynard had an opportunity to discombobulate a scientist who was using one of NASA's fastest and most powerful computers. It was a three-month mission, so the scientist had plenty of time to download, from every database on earth, just about every fact known to man whether scientific, historical, social or political. Maynard monitored the scientist's search on his own screen and could have inserted a comment had he wished but refrained until the scientist asked his computer, "Is there a Supreme Being?" On behalf of the computer, Maynard answered, "There is now."

It also happened that there was considerable downtime on Maynard's spaceflights so he and the crew often had the opportunity to discuss weighty subjects like death and dying. They all hoped if they died in space they would be returned to earth. Maynard was asked, "Do you want to be buried or cremated?" He answered, "Surprise me."

Jeffrey

THE MYTHICAL 98-POUND WEAKLING PORTRAYED in the old Charles Atlas' bodybuilding ads became real when Jeffrey was born. If he stood sideways, you would have trouble seeing him but for his elongated Adam's apple. He was, of course, a 32-year-old computer nerd with his own website offering advice on how to exact revenge. He actually made a nice living out of it but his advice occasionally came back to haunt him.

He told me he got the idea for his website when he was driving out West with his wife and got a flat tire in the Mojave Desert. It was 110 degrees in the shade and he was sweating and swearing a blue streak as he changed the tire. Suddenly, he heard laughter behind him and turned to see a cowboy on his horse amused at his distress. Irrational rage consumed him and he growled to the cowboy, "You think this is funny? You won't think it's so funny when I make you get off that horse and change the tire for me." The cowboy thought about this for a minute and said, "Let me tell you somethin, pardner. Not only am I not gonna change your tire, I'm gonna fuck your wife and you're gonna hold my balls to keep 'em from hittin' the hot sand." A few hours later, as he was driving down the highway, Jeffrey said to his wife, "I really showed that son-of-a-bitch, didn't I? Did you hear him scream when I dropped his balls in the sand?"

Jeffrey was a virgin without any sexual experience at all when he married. The more his commitment to computers, the less his interest in intercourse. He actually didn't know how to do it, so his new wife took him to the doctor for a dispassionate explanation. Try as he might the doctor could not make him understand, so he finally said, "Here, let me show you." He lifted Jeffrey's wife onto the examining table and made clinical love to her. When they were finished, he asked Jeffrey, "Now do you see how it's done?" Jeffrey said, "I do, but I can only bring her in Tuesdays and Fridays."

Sometimes the victim of Jeffrey's advice would try to find him and exact revenge. I was watching one night when he got roaring drunk at a local bar, and a victim put a plastic eyeball in his drink when he went to the bathroom. When he got back, he chug-a-lugged the drink so fast I had no chance to warn him about the eyeball, and then decided not to mention it since he seemed none the worse for wear. A few days later he was feeling awful and asked me to accompany him to the doctor. The doctor took x-rays of him and could find nothing wrong so he asked Jeffrey to climb up on the examining table on all fours so he could examine him. The doctor walked behind him, took a look, and said, "You know, Jeffrey, if you want me to help you, we're going to have to trust each other."

It happens Jeffrey's website had its up and downs. After one very bad year Jeffrey told his wife they had to cut down on expenses. He said they would have to cancel their vacation to Europe, summer camp for the kids, and the new car on order. He also said they would have to reduce household expenses. He told his wife she needed to learn how to clean and launder because they would have to let the maid go. She replied, "That's fine, but you better learn cunnilingus so we can let the pool boy go, too."

Father Snee

FATHER SNEE IS A JESUIT and the living embodiment of Friar Tuck. When he is not teaching agency in law school, he is wearing a Hawaiian shirt and a cowboy hat and riding shotgun with the Ft. Lauderdale sheriff during Easter break. In his early years he was a biblical scholar, but now he visits an Alcohol Rehab facility every six months. It was his profane interpretation of scripture that got him into so much trouble.

As an example, he told me what really happened on Calvary. After Jesus was crucified and night fell, he murmured something on the cross and a soldier climbed a ladder to find out what it was. The soldier's face turned white as Jesus whispered, then he walked into the crowd and called for someone named "Peter." When Peter identified himself, the soldier told him the guy on the cross wanted to speak to him. Peter climbed the ladder, listened, went ashen, returned to the crowd, and was immediately surrounded by disciples pleading to know what their Lord and Master had said. Peter solemnly replied, "He said to me, Peter... Peter... I can see your house from here."

He also told me about an event that occurred at the pearly gates. Jesus relieved Peter who had been on the gates for 1,000 years without a break. While Jesus was standing there, an old man approached him and told him he was looking for his son. Jesus asked for more information about the son. The old man said, "The last time I saw him, he had holes in his hands and feet." Jesus gasped, "Father?" The old man cried, "Pinocchio?"

A second event that occurred at the pearly gates, according to Father Snee, was the time an eminent surgeon, not wanting to wait on the long entrance line, pleaded with Peter for early entrance into heaven based on his eminent career and the thousands of lives he saved. He was turned down. While fuming in line, another doctor wearing a white jacket and carrying a medical bag walked up to the gates and was admitted immediately. The surgeon rushed forward demanding to know why the other doctor was given priority. Peter explained, "That wasn't a doctor. That was God. He thinks he's a doctor."

A third event that occurred at the pearly gates was the time two very, very avid golfers showed up unexpectedly. One was 65 and one was 35 and a bolt of lightning had killed them both on the golf course. Peter consulted his files and said to the 35-year-old, "There's been a terrible mistake. You're early. You shouldn't be here yet. You can go back as anything you want other than your old self. What would you like to go back as?" The 35-year-old thought about it and said, "A pussy with a 3-handicap."

Finally, Father Snee told me about the time he was hitchhiking in civvies to a retreat and was picked up by a beautiful stewardess who appeared desperately horny. She begged him to have sex with her. Caring deeply for a lost soul and wanting to help, he agreed, but only to anal sex. When they were finished, he said to her, "You know, I'm really a priest." She replied, "That's okay, I'm Jack and I'm on my way to a costume party."

Carlton

CARLTON IS THE EXCEPTIONALLY HANDSOME CEO of a Fortune 500 company. He is smooth in discourse; witty in repartee; supremely polished interacting with both board members and customers; and disarmingly charming when required. He believes corporations exist for the enrichment of management; that almost any depredation can be justified by the cliché, "It's in the best interests of shareholders;" that the concept "one hand washes the other" should govern when board members and management set compensation for each other; that the phrase "I was only doing my job" is sufficient to excuse any malefaction; that there are at least five other executives in the company who could do his job as well as he for far less compensation; and that the shareholders are not really owners of the company but just passers-by who could care less about the employees, customers and suppliers.

One night, Carlton attended a retirement party for an Executive VP, got roaring drunk, and made an ass of himself insulting the Chairman of the Board. After the party Carlton's wife told him the Chairman fired him and Carlton said, "Screw him!" His wife replied, "Don't forget your briefcase tomorrow."

Carlton wanted to bribe a big customer with a yacht to keep his business. The customer was offended and said not only his personal ethics but also the conflict-of-interest policy at his company precluded accepting such a gift. Being fast on his feet, Carlton said, "Why don't I sell it to you for $100?" The customer considered that and said, "How about two for the price of one?"

That same year, on a business trip to New York, Carlton was drinking in an upscale bar when a hooker approached him and said she could take him to the moon and back for $1,000. Loving to negotiate, he thought he would see what kind of concessions he could wring from her, so he offered her $500, then $700, then $900, but she held firm at a $1,000. He said, "You know, for $1,000 you would have to do anything I can describe in three words." She accepted the challenge and assured him she was completely uninhibited and would do whatever he wanted. He said, "Paint my townhouse."

The CEO of another company, who Carlton secretly despised and tried to one-up on every occasion, called Carlton and invited him to go for a drive in his new Mercedes –Maybach S600. Carlton sat next to him as he tooled down the highway and waxed eloquent about the car's extra legroom; 523-hp, 6.0 liter, twin-turbo V-12 engine; hot-stone massaging leather recliners; and signature fragrance. The CEO was dripping with condescension when he asked, "Ever ride in one of these before?" Carlton responded patronizingly, "Never in front."

Carlton was also a bit of a sadist so when a mistress with deep-seated masochistic tendencies pleaded with him, "Beat me! Beat Me!" he smirked, "No, I won't."

Roderick

RODERICK IS WITHOUT A DOUBT the raunchiest gynecologist on Manhattan's Park Avenue. It is amazing he chose that specialty since his sordid view of female genitalia is so profane. One must assume that when he is with a patient he is as respectful, considerate, and concerned as is appropriate for a practitioner of the medical arts. But when he is with 'the guys", his humor is ribald and his observations pungent. It is completely inconsistent with his otherwise empathetic and learned image.

He told me there were five gynecological events that influenced his thinking. The first occurred when he married a naïve virgin and discovered on their wedding night that she was unfamiliar with proper feminine hygiene and smelled a bit gamey. He told her about the wonderful products available at the drugstore and urged her to go shopping the next day. When she returned, he asked her how it went, and she said, "It was unbelievable. I had no idea what was available. They had orange douches, lemon douches, even grape douches." He asked, "What did you get?" She chirped, "Tuna!"

The second gynecological event occurred when a lady friend of his complained about a recent date that turned out poorly. She had enjoyed a lovely dinner with a slow but gorgeous southern boy and suggested they view the Manhattan skyline from the New Jersey cliffs. They got into some pretty heavy petting and she pleaded with him breathlessly, "Kiss me where it smells bad." So he drove her to Secaucus.

The third gynecological event occurred when a lovely coed came into his office for her annual checkup. As she took off her clothes Roderick noticed she had a large red welt on her chest in the shape of the letter "H." She explained she was dating a Harvard letterman, horseplay led to sex, he was wearing his sweater, and she was allergic. Roderick gave her some salve. A year later her large red welt was a "Y." Same story: Yale letterman, horseplay, sex, sweater, allergy, salve. Astonishingly, a year later her large red welt was an "M." Amazed, Roderick said, "Let me guess. Michigan!" Bewildered, she replied, "No, Wisconsin!"

The fourth gynecological event occurred when a lovely but upset biology professor he was probing too roughly told him about the first humans. It seems after Mother Nature designed man and woman, she decided to take a nap but before drifting off some nymphs came to her and said, "We're not sure the people you made are complete. They seem to have no sex organs. What genitalia do you want us to put on which person?" Mother Nature thought about it and said, "Put the prick on the dumb one."

The fifth gynecological event occurred when Roderick was in his cups and was asked by one of his fellow practitioners at a medical symposium what the difference was between a baseball and Medusa, the winged female demon with a hideous face and snakes for hair. Roderick thought about it and said, "You know, if you're really, really desperate, and you really, really have to, you can eat the baseball."

Sheila

SHE IS KNOWN AS "SHEILA the Soothsayer" and she is the real deal: caftan, turban, dusty parlor, crystal ball, Ouija board, tea leaves, tarot cards, and stout at 40. How she keeps a straight face as she dispenses her nonsense I will never know but she loves to "set em' up and knock em' down."

She told me a true believer came to see her one day and asked what it would be like for him after death. She consulted her crystal ball and said, "Each morning you will make love. Then you will make love before and after lunch. Then you will make love at mid-day. Then you will make love before and after dinner. Finally, you will make love before going to sleep. The believer asked, "And I'll be an angel in heaven?" She replied, "No, you'll be a rabbit in Chattanooga."

On another occasion, a loud and pushy wife visited Sheila's shop and wanted to know if her elderly husband had made a will and if he was going to leave her anything. Sheila checked the tea leaves at the bottom of the cup and said, "Yes, he made a will which leaves you everything on condition that you remarry." The wife asked, "Why does he care if I remarry?" Sheila checked the tea leaves again and said, "He wants there to be at least one person in the world who regrets his death."

Another week an expectant but obnoxious mother came to see Sheila and wanted to know if she would give birth successfully and if her baby would be beautiful. Sheila flipped over some tarot cards one by one and commented after each; "This card shows you will be in labor a long time. This card shows you will have an emergency C-section. And this card shows you will need many blood transfusions." The expectant woman cried out, "But will the birth be successful? Will my baby be beautiful?" Sheila flipped over the last card and said, "Yes, I see visitors bringing bananas for your chimp."

A frustrated young man visited Sheila and told her he was getting absolutely nowhere with a beautiful girl he was dating and was suffering mightily from repressed sexual desire. He asked if there was lovemaking with her in his future. Sheila moved her Ouija board in circles and gave him this advice: "Take your girl into Tiffany's this Friday and buy her a $50,000 diamond ring. Pay for it with a personal check and say you'll be back Monday to pick it up after its been sized. When you return on Monday the salesman will be furious that your check bounced and you will apologize and leave." The young man asked, "What good will that do?" Sheila answered, "You're going to have one hell of a weekend."

A sleaze insulted Sheila when he asked for the best whorehouse in town. She looked into her crystal ball and recommended he go to Madam Elroy's for the best "wax job" on the planet. She said, "A beautiful girl with an incredible body will give you a blowjob and just before you come will grab your cock and twist it." "And this will give me a great orgasm?" he asked. "No," she said. "It will blow the wax right out of your ears."

Ralph

IF YOU ARE HAVING TROUBLE with your car, you want Ralph to fix it. He has no college education, not even a high school degree, but he has a natural born understanding of machinery. True, he has trouble grasping the subtleties and nuances of esoteric pursuits such as art, politics, economics and philosophy, but he can tell you who won the World Series in 1941 and which one of 25 beers is the Bud. Even covered in grease, he looks and acts like a naive 28-year-old farm boy.

Ralph worked for days on a Maserati owned by a noted heart surgeon. It was a really lengthy and complicated job and put him behind schedule on all the other cars he was repairing. When the surgeon came in to pick up the car, he had to ask, "You know, Doc, there's something I don't understand. We both work on complicated machinery. It took us years to learn what we know. And we both have to be super careful when we take things apart. How come you make so much more money than me doing the same thing?" The surgeon replied quietly, " Try doing it with the engine running."

Ralph and his friend Arnie both groused about the pay disparity between the mechanics and the foreman in the shop. Ralph decided to confront the foreman, who was leaning against a wall reading a tech manual, and ask him why. The foreman said, "I'll show you why. It's a matter of common sense. Punch my hand." He held his hand up and as Ralph threw the punch the foreman pulled it away at the last second and Ralph hit the wall hard. Returning to Arnie in pain, he said, "I'll show you why he makes the big bucks." Ralph held his hand up in front of his face and said, "Punch my hand."

Ralph could not get over the arrogance, conceit and materialism of certain sports car owners. No matter how nice he tried to be to them, they treated him with indifference if not contempt: particularly the Porsche owner who just picked up his car. Ralph observed to Arnie as he drove away, "Do you know what the difference is between a Porsche and a porcupine?" Arnie said "No, what?" Ralph replied, "With a porcupine all the pricks are on the outside."

Another sports car owner brought in his car straight from an accident where a passing truck had ripped off the door of his Mercedes SL 550. He complained to Ralph, "Do you see what that asshole did to my car?" Ralph was amazed he could think about the car when his arm had been ripped off at the elbow. He pointed this out and the owner screamed, "God damn it, I've lost my Piaget, too!"

Finally, when he was on tow truck duty, Ralph was asked to help a driver whose car had broken down under a bridge. When he got to the scene of the accident it was not a car, it was a truck, and it did not break down under the bridge, it was wedged under the bridge. There was also a line of cars backed up for two miles or so because of the mishap. Ralph went up to the truck driver and said, "Got stuck, huh?" The driver looked at him for a moment and said, "No, I was delivering the bridge and ran out of gas."

Georgina

GEORGINA IS A GOSSIP COLUMNIST and a first-class, no-nonsense, nasty bitch. She takes no prisoners and neither gives quarter nor asks it. Her clothing is severe, her hair butch, her glasses steel, her pumps stiletto, and her jewelry spare. She claims 37; concedes 44; and is pushing 50. She believes the secret to never growing old is to be nasty with just about everyone; particularly those who suck up to you, and those who to claim to eat healthy, get plenty of sleep, exercise regularly, and then lie about their age.

She was lunching with some girlfriends one day at a very expensive restaurant in Beverly Hills and recounting her date the night before with a famous actor who believed he was not only God's gift to women, but a superb lover as well. Her girlfriends were keen to know how it went and urged her to share what happened. She recounted, "We had a nice evening. We went to Spago's, I ordered the trout almandine, we went to his place, he made his move, et cetera, et cetera, and I left after breakfast." One girlfriend complained, "But you skipped over the most exciting part!" "No," Georgina explained examining her nails, "I mentioned the trout almandine."

When the ladies left the restaurant there was a mime in the street faking the opening and closing of a door so Georgina went up to his tip cup and faked putting in $5.

As the ladies strolled down the street an obvious out-of-towner from the sticks came up to them and went on and on about how expensive everything was in Beverly Hills. She asked, "Do you know where I can see some cheap clothing?" Georgina replied, "How about your reflection in that window?"

Sadly, Georgina's first husband died an untimely death. She had been mistakenly feeding him dog food for over a month. It was not really her fault. She usually had an assistant shop for her and was unfamiliar with brand names and packaging and product placement inside the supermarket. By the time her assistant returned from vacation, her husband had died and her assistant was shocked to learn what Georgina had been feeding him. She asked, "Did he die because of the dog food?" Georgina replied, "No, he broke his back trying to lick his balls."

Her assistant returned from the vacation loving both the food and the activities, but the social and sexual aspects had gone poorly because all the men she met turned out to be narcissistic. She asked Georgina, "How can you know if someone's stuck up?" Georgina answered, "He'll usually fantasize he's someone else when fucking."

Georgina also decided to publish a story in her column that she heard from reliable sources about an actor who was vain beyond belief and considered himself to be incredibly well-hung. According to the story, he went into a doctor's office, took out his penis, and banged it down on the doctor's desk. He crowed, "Doc, look at that!" The doctor said, "There's nothing wrong with that." He gushed, "I know. Isn't it great!"

Part 4

Milton

IF YOU HAVE BEEN WATCHING cable news recently, you know Milton is a television commentator. Upon meeting him one is reminded of that great line from *My Fair Lady*: "Oiling his way around the floor, oozing charm from every pore..." He is the perfect front man for his ratings-obsessed TV network because of his indifference to suffering and humiliation as well as his penchant for sensationalizing the mundane, alarming without justification, ambushing to embarrass, and smiling while assassinating.

Before becoming a newscaster, Milton was a television producer. He would do anything "the talent" wanted: they were the stars that made the industry prosper. He would ensure they had their own car and driver; that their trailer was carpeted and wood-paneled; that they flew only first class or by private jet; and that their meals were catered by the finest restaurants. He was so smooth they would only learn their shows had been cancelled when his limousine dropped them off at the unemployment office.

His great regret was his inability to convince others he was an erudite and thoughtful TV host who moderated intelligent debates among the wise and powerful on various discussion panels. It seems there was always a smart ass or dumb ass or sarcastic ass or pompous ass on the panel who would crush his image with just the wrong phrase at just the wrong time.

For example, I sat in on one of his panels debating religion versus atheism and the human need for a deity. Historical precedents, biblical quotations and devotional practices were hotly debated until an actress opined, "Atheism won't work. Whose name are you going to scream when you have an orgasm?"

Another panel discussed new financial opportunities in the marketplace, particularly the establishment of banks for women. A comedienne observed, "I won't bank there. It's closed too many days a month for cramps."

Then there was the panel that discussed the need in society for sex magazines as an outlet for aggression. A centerfold was held up showing a woman whose breasts were covered with whip cream. A rabbi on the panel confessed, "I use non-dairy creamer. My wife's breasts are silicone."

It got even worse with a panel on contraception. The various methods of condoms versus pills versus abstention were discussed at length. It was agreed the *morning after* pill worked best and someone inquired if it were possible to develop one for men? Milton asked the panel, "Do you think they would need one?" One wise guy answered, "Yes, to change their blood type."

Finally, three gynecologists debated the risks of being overly intimate when examining women. Milton asked, "Because of lawsuits?" "No," one of them smirked, "herpes!"

Rufus

HE TAKES AN APPLE WITHOUT paying from the fruit stand. His wears his gun belt below his beer belly. He eats lunch for free at the diner. He cat-naps during stakeouts. And he looks the other way for minor infractions. He is your typical, middle-aged, world-weary, cop on the beat. He is Rufus: the long arm of the law; the first responder; the protector in blue. Sometimes the advice he gives is less than perfect.

He arrested Herbert the Flasher on nine separate occasions. In the beginning he tried to counsel him that his lewd behavior had to stop, and Herbert would swear it was the last time and he would never do it again. Then, a month or two would go by and the complaints would start again. Rufus finally arrested Herbert in the dead of winter. The poor guy was so cold he could not stop shivering. He said, "Wh-wh-what am I g-g-gonna d-do? Help m-me, I'm d-desperate. I c-can't get w-warm." Rufus replied, "Why don't you just describe yourself instead of opening your coat?"

Rufus was part of the team investigating a kidnapping. He was in the living room of the home of the kidnapped teenager when the call came in demanding an exorbitant ransom or else the kid's body parts would start showing up in the mail. The father refused and a week later when Rufus was on duty a package arrived with the kid's thumb in it. The mother groaned in agony and to comfort her Rufus said, "Don't worry. We'll reassemble him once we have all the parts."

On another occasion, Rufus and I were eating near the entrance of a Chinese restaurant when a thief came in with a gun and shouted he wanted everything in the cash register. Rufus responded, on behalf of the owner, "Is that for here or to go?"

In his younger days, Rufus talked down a jumper who wanted to commit suicide by leaping off a seven-story building. The jumper said, "I can't take it any more! I've been in therapy for ten years and nothing is helping." Rufus inquired, "With a strict or lenient thera-pist?" The jumper said, "Strict. Why?" Rufus said, "You might as well come in. He'll charge you for missing an appointment."

Shortly afterward, Rufus was called to a five-alarm fire at a hotel and was helping the guests evacuate when a naked man carrying his clothes ran up to him and exclaimed, "Have you seen a raven-haired beauty with an incredible body come out of the hotel?" Rufus said, "No. Is that your wife? Do you want me to find her and bring her to you?" The man said, "No, screw her. I prepaid for it."

Then, last year, Rufus and his partner were called to assist a little old man who had been sitting on a park bench for three days. As they approached they could see he was crying and when they asked why, he said he had just married a beautiful 24-year-old girl who was filthy rich and incredible in bed. Rufus's partner whispered to him, "Why is he crying?" and Rufus whispered back, "He probably can't remember his address."

Vlad

THE LITTLE KIDS CALL HIM "Vlad the Undertaker." He prefers "Skilled Mortician." You might picture him as thin, gaunt, morose, droopy-eyed and dressed in black and this time you would be right. He lives the part; he loves the part. But his insensitivity to the suffering of the bereaved is impressive.

He started his career in Appalachia and the hooch and feuds of the hillbillies kept his business humming. The problem with such customers, however, was that wills were few and far between and the hillbillies rarely documented which heirs should inherit what property. Thus, there were many burial delays and location changes as the probate courts sorted through competing claims. In one instance, a hillbilly did establish a trust for his wife but she complained about it continuously and Vlad's assistant wondered why? Vlad observed, "She can't inherit until she's 13."

I first met Vlad when he became a cemetery superintendent. I was touring the cemetery's grounds with him when an enraged man named Schultz confronted him and complained someone had peed the words "Fuck Schultz" in the snow on his family plot. Vlad calmed the man by promising to get to the bottom of it. After investigating, he called the man and said, "I have good news for you and bad news for you." The man asked, "What's the good news?" Vlad replied, "We found the culprit. It was one of the groundskeepers." The man said, "Okay, what's the bad news?" Vlad replied, "It was in your wife's handwriting."

Often, Vlad would help the bereaved write obituaries for their loved ones. A very feisty woman arrived at his office one day riding her deceased husband's Harley-Davidson and asked him for help with her husband's obituary. Vlad surmised she was not all that unhappy about his death. He asked for the essence of what she wanted to say, and she replied, "Smoot is dead." Vlad said, "I'm sorry, but the newspaper requires at least six words." She asked, "What do you suggest?" He thought about it and said, "How about, 'Smoot is dead. Harley for sale!'"

A man came into Vlad's funeral home and said, "I'd like to make arrangements to bury my wife." Vlad said, "We can help you, most assuredly," and they reviewed all the coffin and internment and floral choices available to the bereaved. After a while, Vlad said, "Do you know, I think we've met before." The man said, "Actually, we have. You helped me bury my first wife. I remarried." "Really?" Vlad said, "Congratulations!"

In church one day before a funeral, Vlad decided to get on the confessional line behind four nuns. The acoustics were such that those waiting in line could hear what was said in the booth. For a finger on the penis, the first nun got three Hail Mary's and a finger swish in the holy water. For a hand on the penis, the second nun got six Hail Mary's and a hand swish in the holy water. The fourth nun whispered urgently to Vlad, "Do you think Father Riley will let me gargle the holy water before Sister Anne sits in it?"

Scott

Scott is a commercial airline pilot and captains some of the biggest jets in the fleet. Prior to that, he had an illustrious career flying combat missions in Iraq. When you see him standing on the tarmac clear-eyed, graying, ruddy, fit, and dedicated, you can almost hear *America the Beautiful* playing softly in the background. If only he could suppress his inner Puck, he might one day qualify for senior management.

He loves to take junior pilots under his wing and mentor them in the refinements of flying. He helps them acclimate to the routine by observing, "This is the definition is of a good flight: The Second Officer gets laid, the First Officer has a good night's sleep, and the Captain has a good crap."

His fixation on bowel movements does not stop there. When advising newbies on the etiquette of sex among the crew, he warns, "Never forget. On a long flight, there is nothing so overrated as a good lay or so underrated as a good dump."

Passengers are not exempt from the mockery of his humor. I was on one of his flights when he came over the intercom and said, "Ladies and

Gentlemen, welcome to our morning flight from Los Angeles to New York. You are on one of the newest and fastest jetliners in the sky. Every precaution has been taken for your comfort and safety including a vast array of redundant and automated systems. So sit back and relax and take comfort in the knowledge that everything is working perfectly... everything is working perfectly... everything is working perfectly..."

Airline employees at the check-in counter are also his victims. One day he wanted to check some extra luggage on his flight so he went up to the girl at the counter and said, "I'd like to send this suitcase to Rome, this one to Johannesburg, and this one to Tokyo." The girl said, "We can't do that." He said, "Why not? You did it yesterday."

He also likes to be deceptive when flying as a passenger to his next assignment. On one flight, he was really suffering from gas and could not help himself and cut a huge one. It was extraordinarily loud and malodorous and passengers all around looked up and stared at him. He calmly turned around and stared at the passenger behind him.

Early in his career Scott flew some cargo charters. He told me about one really strange flight where he was asked to transport some seagulls from Seattle to San Diego to feed some very sick porpoises. Apparently, someone had convinced the owner of the porpoises, which starred in an aquarium show, that the seagulls had special nutrients that would make the porpoises immortal. The owner joined Scott's flight. I asked, "How did it work out?" Scott answered, "Not so good. The owner was arrested." Surprised, I asked, "On what grounds?" Scott replied, "He was arrested for transporting gulls across state lines for immortal porpoises." I groaned. He smirked, "But he did eat well. When I gave him two choices for dinner, he asked, 'What are they?' and I replied, 'Yes and no.'"

Ernie

ERNIE IS A CAR SALESMAN. Picture a gorgeous actor. Then, hold the hair, hold the smile, hold the complexion, hold the physique, hold the dimples, hold the eyes, hold the youth, hold the talent and hold the ambition. Keep the cynicism.

He was working at a luxury-car dealership when a rube rolled in looking for a new car and flashing a roll of $10,000 bills that would choke a horse. When the rube said he intended to pay cash, Ernie took a special interest and escorted him around the showroom trying to figure out what he could say that would impress the yokel on his own terms. The rube sat in a convertible and asked if he could take it for a test drive, so Ernie reached into his pocket for the keys and brought out some golf tees as well. The rube asked, "What are those for?" Ernie replied, "They're to rest your balls on when driving." Amazed, the rube exclaimed, "Those Mercedes people think of everything!"

He started out working at a used-car lot. That is where we met. The owner would not give him a permanent job until he proved he could sell. First, he moved a lemon with two flat tires. Second, he sold a convertible with a ripped top. Third, he conveyed a car whose floorboards were rusted. Fourth, he waived goodbye as a buyer towed a wreck into the street. And fifth, he sold the oldest car on the lot, by far. The owner was impressed and gave him one more test. He said, "Sell that ugly, useless, outdated jalopy over there and the job is yours." Ten minutes later Ernie slammed the bill of sale for the jalopy on the owner's desk. The owner said, "Wow! How did you do it?" Ernie smiled and said, "Once I hid the Seeing Eye Dog, the sale was easy."

Ernie also liked to tease a rather dimwitted but likable mechanic on the lot named Stuart. One morning Stuart was having trouble starting a car. Ernie said, "You'll have to jump it, but don't get your balls between the positive and negative terminals."

Another time, Ernie borrowed a loaner and got roaring drunk between the dealership and his apartment. Driving home he hit a tree, backed up, hit it again, backed up, hit it again, backed up, etc., etc. The next day he swore he got lost in a forest.

An apprentice mechanic on the lot, who hoped to own his own shop one day, asked Ernie, "Which is the best trade school to go to?" Ernie said, "Forget school. Just open the hood, sigh, cluck your tongue, and say softly, 'Oh, my God.'"

Lastly, Ernie took Stuart on a camping trip deep in the woods to reward his helpful work. Unfortunately, a rattlesnake bit Stuart on the tip of his penis and he begged Ernie to get medical help. After hiking miles to cell coverage, Ernie asked a doctor what to do and the doctor said, "You have to suck the venom out of the fang holes." Ernie said, "Really?" "The doctor said, "Absolutely!" So Ernie trudged back up the road, trekked through miles of forest and streams, and finally reached Stuart who was on his last legs. Stuart gasped, "What did the doctor say?" Ernie said, "You're going to die."

Rita

Rita is a hooker. She lives in San Francisco with her son, but needing extra money to make ends meet, she works the beat in Las Vegas every other weekend. No one at the real estate agency where she works in San Francisco knows about her moonlighting activities. Because she is young and beautiful, she does not do multiple tricks per night unless the money is spectacular, but prefers a full night's commitment and charges accordingly. She brings both wit and wisdom to the job.

Rita attended the wedding of a well-known Jewish-American Princess in Las Vegas whom she knew as a child, and brought a fellow hooker along as her guest. It was a lovely ceremony and of considerable interest to her friend because she had never attended a Jewish wedding before. She loved the tradition and the ceremony and was struck by the radiant smile on the bride's face, particularly as she came down the aisle. She asked Rita, "Why is she smiling so much?" Rita answered, "She knows her blow job days are over."

Rita was also invited to participate in a swingers' orgy but was advised not to come alone so she asked me to accompany her as her "partner." One of her co-workers who had also been invited decided not to attend the orgy when she heard a lot of strangers would be there whom she did not know. I asked Rita, "Why is that?" and she said, "She only likes to see faces at orgies that she's sat on."

In very much the same spirit, Rita told me about a self-styled lothario who prowled Las Vegas bars asking strange women if they wanted to play *Circus*? I asked, "What if the woman asks how to play?" Rita replied, "Then, he says, 'You sit on my face and I guess your weight.'"

Another come-on question she frequently hears is, "Hey, baby, want to play *Rodeo*?" I asked, "How do you play that?" She replied, "The guy mounts the woman from behind, tells her she feels just like her mother, and tries to hold on for eight seconds."

On one particular visit to Las Vegas, Rita had time to go to a sporting goods store to buy a baseball glove for her son. As she browsed the aisles, she realized her son might also like a baseball bat but she did not have enough cash on her and did not want to leave an electronic trail with a credit card. As she finished browsing, the salesman asked, "Wanna ball for the glove?" and she said, "No, but I'll blow you for the bat."

Rita also makes it a habit to come well prepared for her encounters because the johns frequently forget to use protection in the excitement of the moment. She carries an assortment of condoms in a box with a little saying printed on the lid, "Condom warehouse. We fit all sizes." One of her customers asked, "Who fits the condoms?" She said, "I do." He said, "Well, could you wash your hands before putting those lemon slices in my gin and tonic?"

Sven

Sᴠᴇɴ ɪs ᴀ sᴋɪ ɪɴsᴛʀᴜᴄᴛᴏʀ without peer. He looks like a swarthy Italian and is built like a fireplug. Thus, when he speaks with a thick Austrian accent and races down the slope with the lightness of a gazelle, his students are justified in being nonplused. Who knows what mixing and matching took place in his lineage? The result, however, was an engaging insouciance at 34.

He taught me to ski and encouraged me to take one of the most satisfying spills I ever had. I was skiing down the beginner's slope making slow and careful turns with him following close behind. At the bottom of the slope, a know-it-all husband was yelling up to his wife, who was also a beginner and skiing ahead of me, "Turn right… okay, now turn left…okay, right again…now left…" The problem was he kept having her turn right in front of me as I was trying to get by and in panicked frustration I yelled to Sven, "What do I do?" He hollered, "Fall down!"…"What?"…"Fall down!" So, I did. It was just like bowling. First, I plowed into her, knocking her over; then, as one, we slid down the hill on our backs, blasting the son-of-a-bitch at the bottom five feet into the air.

On another occasion, three middle-aged women took a private skiing lesson with Sven and he was surprised at how flirtatious they were. In fact, one of them eagerly went to bed with him and was sensational in the sack. When I asked him if it was hard to seduce her, he said, "Not at all. I overheard them talking during lunch when I returned to the table with their food, and they were debating how much to tip me at the end of the ski lesson. One confessed she called her husband and asked him and he said, 'Screw him!'" Sven smiled, "She was a very obedient wife."

Sven befriended a rather slow-witted ski instructor from the sticks and tried to mentor him not only on the finer points of the sport, but on the finer points of sex, because whenever Sven entered the instructors' quarters, the kid was masturbating. Finally, he introduced him to a sweet ski instructor named Jill and they moved in together. A few weeks later Sven caught the kid masturbating again and asked, "What happened to Jill?" The kid answered, "She's resting her arm."

It is a truism that ski instructors are babe magnets. There is something about the crisp, clean air, the blinding snow, and the rush downhill that gets the blood racing. There is also something about the sport that causes older men to bring along younger women. Sven was giving a private lesson to a wealthy art collector and his secretary, Fawn, when the collector received a call on his cell phone. He took the call and was very upset by it. Sven asked him, "Is everything all right?" He answered, "That was my lawyer. He's seen a picture that will cost me $12 million dollars." Sven asked, "Isn't that good?" He answered, "It's of me and Fawn. My wife found it."

I asked Sven over lunch, "Who are the happiest skiers of all? He said, "Alzheimer patients, without doubt." I asked, "Why?" and he said, "Everyone they meet is new."

Mustafa

ONCE A YEAR THEY BALANCE his weight on the scale with gold. At ceremonies, he wears a leopard skin over his three hundred pound frame, and his crown is made of ostrich feathers. He is the beloved chief of the Kumbata tribe and has been so for over 40 years, and his greatest wish is to usher his people into the modern world. With a twinkle in his eye and mirth in his manner, he views life with some cynicism, but is still everyone's jolly uncle.

I met him at a transfer of power ceremony, when the colonial government that held sway over his land was going to transfer sovereignty to his nation. He was dressed in his regalia, the colonial governor was bedecked with chevrons and medals, and the natives were lined up on one side of the presentation pitch and the colonials on the other. As the governor handed Mustafa the gold scepter symbolizing the transfer of power, Mustafa almost dropped it, whereupon a pigmy-sized member of the tribe ran up and down the rows of the assembled women squeezing their breasts as fast as he could. At the reception afterward, I asked Mustafa what that was all about. He said, "Well, our understanding is that in the civilized world when something untoward happens during a formal ceremony, a titter runs through the crowd, and that was our titter."

Another time, when he was visiting New York, he mentioned to me that he just had an unusual visit with a doctor. He went because each time he farted it sounded like, "Honda!" The doctor asked him a battery of questions, particularly about what he recently had to eat and drink. The doctor specifically asked him if he had imbibed any alcohol the last couple of days and he noted he had consumed quite a bit of absinthe. The doctor exclaimed, "Of course, that's it! Absinthe makes the fart go 'Honda!'"

Another time we discussed the benefits and burdens of power. He said he learned some very hard lessons in ordering warriors, or their pages, to their death. Once, a rainbow appeared outside his village and he sent two warriors out to collect the pot of gold. As they reached down to pick it up, two yellow fingers came out of the sky and crushed them to death. In frustration, he sent out two pages and they easily picked up the gold and brought it inside. I asked, "What did you learn from that?" He said ruefully, "Let your pages do the walking through the yellow fingers."

Still another time, when he was visiting New York, I found him sitting on a curb late at night spitting and repeating over and over, "Ptui! What a driver. Ptui! What a driver." I asked him why he was doing that? He said he was on Wall Street and needed to get to midtown for an important meeting so he hopped in a cab driven by a very attractive blonde. The traffic was horrendous and he could not miss the meeting so he decided to hop out and run for it. The driver said, "No, no. I promise I'll get you there in time," and Mustafa said, "Honey, if you can get me there in time, I'll eat every hair on your pussy. Ptui! What a driver."

Lydia

LYDIA TEACHES FIRST GRADE. SHE is the young educator I always wanted but never had: perfect figure, beautiful eyes, lovely smile, pixie hairdo, and loving touch. She wears dresses and heels every day to project an aura of seriousness and formality, and although such characteristics are perceived only dimly by her charges, they are perceived nonetheless. She loves the terribly serious answers that pop out of kids' mouths when asked questions, and deliberately styles her questions to elicit them. She is truly an exploiter of the innocent.

I attended one of her classes as a guest speaker and then remained behind to watch her work with the kids. Her questions brought out their very best:

She said, "Robert, your cat story is the same as your sister's. Did you copy her story?" "No," he shot back. "It's the same cat."

She asked Becky, "How do you spell elephant?" Becky said, "E-L-Y-F-A-N-T!" Lydia replied, "No, that's incorrect," and Becky answered, "Maybe, but you asked how I spelled it."

Seth, who was always tardy, slipped quietly into the classroom. Lydia said to him, "Please tell the class why you're late," and he replied, "You started before I got here."

To Sarah she said, "Can you name something we have today that we didn't have before you were born?" Sarah piped up, "Me."

She asked George, "Why do you always have dirt on your clothes? You don't see any dirt on my clothes?" He answered, "You're a lot farther from the ground than me."

She asked Oscar, "We are told George Washington cut down his Dad's tree and then admitted it. Do you know why his Dad forgave him?" Oscar replied, "He was still holding the axe."

To Marlene she said, "Please spell the word 'water.'" Marlene said proudly, "H-I-J-K-L-M-N-O!" Lydia asked, "Why did you spell it that way?" and Marlene said, "Because you said it was H to O."

To Tyrone she said, "Can you give us a sentence that has the word 'before' in it?" He replied proudly, "Two and two be four."

Finally, she asked Debbie, "Why are you doing your equations on the floor?" And Debbie responded, "You told us not to use tables." And with that, she asked the entire class, "Can you name someone who keeps on talking when nobody else is listening?" And as though they were one, the kids shouted, "A teacher!"

Arlo

ARLO, NOW 38, WRITES SHORT, pithy, classified ads for a living. He tried
his hand at writing a book but lacked the discipline to finish it. His
career as a war correspondent ended prematurely when he was
shot in the ass. He tried his hand at essays and articles but was in-
sufficiently compensated by his intellectual inferiors. Finally, when
stand-up comedy exploiting his cadaver-like mien and wry disposition proved unavailing, he turned to writing jokes, then obituaries,
then finally, classified ads. He kept a double set of books: One containing the actual ads he wrote for customers, the other containing the ads he wished he could have written. He gave me these
examples of the latter:

A customer came to him and asked him to find a way to send a
subtle message to his new wife who regrettably turned out to be
far more unruly and opinionated than he anticipated. He knew she
read the classifieds assiduously and he wanted to use them to send
a message. Arlo asked him if he had any property to sell that his
wife would know about, and he answered in the affirmative. So,
Arlo's private ad read, "Complete World Book Encyclopedia for

sale. Superb condition. Thirty-seven volumes. Only $500. No longer required. New wife knows everything."

For another customer looking to get rid of puppies resulting from the unfortunate mating of a cur with her darling Muffin, Arlo's private ad read, "Five puppies free. Mother a purebred Golden Retriever registered with the American Kennel Club. Father a medal-winning, fence-soaring, high-jumper."

Another customer, a rancher, found himself out $10,000 when a stallion he bought proved uninterested in covering his mares. He also bought several additional fillies and mares in the hope of starting a quality herd, but now the vet and feed bills were killing him. Arlo's private ad read, "Virgin fillies and mares for sale, plus one gay stallion."

Another customer, a disillusioned bride, asked Arlo to help her sell the gifts and gowns she acquired before her wedding. She said she married young and did not know what a cad her fiancé was until it was too late. She hoped her story would be an object lesson for other young girls contemplating marriage. Arlo suggested she sell each item separately to earn the most money. His private ad for one of the gowns read, "For sale. Gorgeous wedding dress. $1,500. Only worn once by mistake."

Another customer, an exasperated dog owner, asked Arlo for help in selling his pet. The animal was hell on wheels chewing furniture, barking at every sound, peeing on the rug, and screwing his neighbor's Cocker Spaniel. Arlo did not think the dog would sell but could probably be given away. His private ad read, "Jack Russell

Terrier available free. Five years old. Spiteful little shit! Bites, barks, screws."

Finally, an author asked Arlo to help sell his book on seduction. Arlo's private ad read, "Help her multitask! Show her how to have sex and a headache at the same time."

Part 5

Victor

IF YOU LOOK BENEATH UNDERPASSES, down alleys, and behind soup kitchens you will find Victor: a career hobo for 55 years. Not an article of his clothing is without holes. Shaves are few and far between. His smile is a crenellated mess and his gray hair is sparse and wild. Yet he is a philosopher king well educated at Choate, Penn and Yale. How he descended into his current station is a tale for another time, but his jaundiced view of life is worth passing on. Here are some observations he shared with me:

"I used to think I was poverty-stricken. Then they told me I wasn't poverty-stricken; I was disadvantaged. Then they told me not to think of myself as disadvantaged; I was impoverished. Then they told me I wasn't impoverished'; I was indigent. Today, I still don't have a penny, but I'm an expert on jargon.

"The trouble with always being poor is not that it's boring; it just takes too much time.

"The medical outcomes for the poor sometimes have unusual results. I was forced to go to a free clinic because of scrotal pain and after examining me closely with cupping, pulling, and compressing, the doctor said, 'I have some bad news for you and some good news for you.' So, I asked him 'What's the bad news?' He said, 'Based on your condition, I think you're gay.' I replied, 'Then, what's the good news?' He said, 'I think you're darling.'

"We were poor when I was a child, but didn't know we were poor until the government told us so.

"For awhile I acted Jewish to obtain supplemental charity, but gave it up after a painful incident. I was in a bar wearing my yarmulke and bitching about Kim Jong-un, the North Korean leader, when I spotted an Asian drinking by himself. I went up to him and decked him. As he got up, he said, 'Why did you do that?' I said, 'That's for the Korean War!' He said, 'But I'm Malaysian.' I said, 'Korean, Malaysian, what's the difference?' Later on, he came over, slugged me, and said, 'Remember the *Titanic*!' I sputtered, 'But the *Titanic* hit an iceberg!' He said, 'Iceberg, Rosenberg, what's the difference?'

"Before I left the bar, I heard a conversation in Russian and went over to the guys who were speaking it and said, 'Don't talk Russian. This is the U.S. Talk Spanish!'

"Lastly, my friends and I used to hang around an XXX-rated video store. A lady from the Salvation Army confronted us one day saying we were wrong to do that and it was corrupting our morals. She also pointed out that our milling about offended public decency. She said, 'I know what you're doing. I rented one of those disgusting videos and had to sit through oral sex, anal sex, multiple-partner sex, and even animal sex. Come to our mission and be cleansed. Come to our mission and be saved. Any questions?' We shouted as one, 'What's the name of that video?'"

Sasha

SASHA INSISTS HE IS NEITHER transsexual nor transgender. He is a trans-vestite to the bone and prefers the appellation "cross-dresser." Marilyn Monroe was his idol and he mimics her with every dress, pose, smile, and affectation. He does draw the line at having his skirt blown into the air by a gust of wind, as the resulting "tell" might prove awkward. But many, many men who picked him up and invited him to their bed rued the day they were taken in by his allurements. Sasha is philosophical about his sexual and sartorial preferences and endures society's displeasure with equanimity.

I was with him when he entered an upscale Beverly Hills boutique and decided to look for the *perfect* cocktail dress. He tried on one after another until the clerk was frazzled. Then, spotting a low-cut item near the sales counter, he insisted on trying it on and needed my help getting into it. He twirled in front of the mirror model-ing it from every angle and gushed, "I think this dress displays my breasts wonderfully." A passing shopper muttered, "I didn't know chest hair was this year's *must*."

Sasha had several jobs working in fashionable boutiques as well as sports outlets. At one of the latter, a young woman came in looking for a jockstrap for her boyfriend. Sasha displayed jockstraps in several different colors and sizes. The young woman picked gray. As for sizes, she said "No" when Sasha's raised his pinkie, then "No" to two raised fingers, then "No" to three raised fingers, and then "No" to four raised fingers, Finally, the woman said, "Add the thumb and I think you've got it." Sasha did so, inserted all five fingers in his mouth, and declared, "He's a large."

We often had drinks at a nearby cocktail lounge and more often than not Sasha would leave me to drink alone when his *come hither* looks attracted a likely swain. Unfortunately, Sasha was used to, and preferred, very well-hung men and often rejoined me quickly at the bar when his expectations were unfulfilled. On one occasion when he returned early, I asked him, "How did it go?" He said, "Not so well. We went to a dark, back room and made out like crazy. I was getting more and more turned on when he unzipped his trousers and put something in my hand and I destroyed the moment by saying, 'No, thanks. Cigarettes make me cough.'"

Sasha loved to attend formal balls and to dress up as elegantly as he could. He asked me to accompany him to one of the balls and I had to admit his gown was stunning and he looked fetching. We were dancing a rhumba when one of his earrings came loose and dropped down the back of his dress. Wiggle as he might, he could not shake it free so when a fox trot was played, he asked me to put my hand down the back of his dress and retrieve it. As we danced and I fumbled around down there, the dancers around us looked askance and I said to Sasha, "This is no good. I feel a perfect ass. " Sasha said, "Skip the flattery. Find my earring."

And per Sasha, "Heterosexuality is overrated. Birth is a sexually transmitted disease."

Ted

TED BLOOM IS ADEPT AT public speaking and tours the country as a spokesman for a large insurance company. He is naturally shy, so his chosen profession makes little sense until you realize his wit makes up for his reticence and self-effacement. If you were old enough, you would say he resembles Wally Cox, the TV personality. If not, he is just a skinny; glasses-wearing, soft-spoken, short little guy about 40 who wears suits one size too small. He loves to open his talks with "on-the-road" stories to warm up the audience. Here are a few I remember:

In Philadelphia, he said, "Last night, when it was snowing heavily, I arrived in town for today's speaking engagement and was accompanied by my lovely young aide who I suspected had a crush on me. We arrived very late and the hotel that held our reservation had only one twin-bed room left due to a booking error. Because it was so late, and I did not want to go back into the storm, I decided to take the room and my aide raised no objection. In the middle of the night she cooed to me, 'Mr. Bloom, it's awfully cold in here.' I replied, 'Robin would you like to play my wife tonight?' She said,

'I'd love that.' So I said, 'Then get out of bed and close the god-damned window.'"

In Miami, he opened with, "I arrived in town yesterday afternoon after a very long flight and had dinner with a candidate for a job as my secretary. I knew almost immediately that if I hired her it would be for her proficiency, not her looks. We went to a very fancy restaurant and perused the menu. She said, 'Can I have anything I want?' I replied, 'What do you have in mind?' She said, 'I guess the filet mignon.' I said, 'Guess again.'"

In Tucson, he opened with, "When I arrived at my hotel today, I had an urgent message to call one of the insurance adjusters at my company. I did so immediately and was told my house was badly damaged in a severe storm. I was stunned but not really unhappy because I never liked the house to begin with. I said, 'Okay, send me the cash value right away so I can build a new house.' He said, 'Unfortunately, you had a replacement policy and we can only restore it to what it was.' I reflected on that and said, 'If you check my file you'll see I bought a policy on my wife. Cancel it.'"

In Portland, he opened with, "I had a real shock this morning before I left the office because some of my co-workers pulled me into a conference room to plot a revolution. It seems they felt the CEO of our company, who was out of town, was too old and senile to do his job. We were interrupted by a call from the CEO's assistant saying he had returned early from his trip and was heading toward the conference room. I barked, "If he sees us here, he'll know we're plotting. Jump out the window!' The ringleader shot back, "From the thirteenth floor?' I yelled, 'Forget the superstition. Jump, dammit!"

In Dubuque, he said, "This morning I got a call from my wife saying we had a new baby. I asked, 'Little boy or little girl?' She said, 'Ted, is sex all you ever think about?'"

Harry

WHEN HARRY RETIRED FROM THE Navy he had attained the rank of rear admiral and on two occasions commanded a battle group comprised of a carrier, two cruisers, two destroyers, a frigate, two submarines and a supply ship. He saw combat in Syria, Afghanistan, Iraq, and Vietnam and provided naval support for conflicts in Libya, Yemen and Somalia. It is amazing he rose so high in the Navy because he simply could not resist playing career-ending practical jokes.

Many years ago, I was serving with him on the bridge of the battleship USS Missouri that was sailing along the U.S. east coast. He was familiar with the waters. That could not be said of the captain, who had spent most of his career in the Far East. One night, Harry urgently called the captain to the bridge saying they appeared to be on a collision course with another ship. The captain radioed the other ship, "Please change your course 15 degrees north." The reply came back, "Change your course 15 degrees south." The captain radioed in a louder voice, "I am the captain of this ship. Please change your course immediately to 15 degrees north." The reply came back, "I really think you should proceed 15 degrees south." The furious captain screamed, "I'm in command of the battleship Missouri. Change course, now!" The calm reply came back, "I'm sitting in a lighthouse. Your move."

On another occasion, when Harry was serving late at night as officer of the watch and was buried under charts and reports, a slightly woozy admiral and captain came to him and asked him to settle a bet. The admiral said, "Lieutenant, we've been arguing whether screwing is work or pleasure. What do you think?" Upon reflection, Harry said, "I think it is pleasure, sir." The admiral asked, "Why is that?" Harry replied, "Because if it was work, I'd be doing it."

Then, there was the time Harry addressed the ladies at a Navy Wives of America luncheon and decided to tell some ethnic jokes. He asked, "How does a Polish firing squad work?" No response. "They stand in a circle." Silence. He asked, "When does an Italian parachute open?" No response. "On impact." Silence. He asked, "What happens when Arab and Israeli tanks collide?" No response. "The Arabs throw open the hatch and yell, 'I surrender! I surrender!' The Israelis throw open the hatch and yell, 'Whiplash! Whiplash!'" Silence. Finally, he asked, "Why do French troops come skulking back from the front after their commander urges them 'On to Glory!' No response. "They couldn't find Glory on the map." Maybe a chortle.

Harry and another junior officer who was a farm boy from the midwest were struggling to keep their footing as their destroyer pitched and rolled in a severe tropical storm. The farm boy said, "This is nothing. The winds in my state can topple silos." Harry countered, smiling, "I'm a farm boy, too, and in my state the winds are so strong a goose can lay the same egg five times."

Billy

BILLY EARNED HIS SHOE SALESMAN'S stripes at Neiman's, Nordstrom's, Macy's and Bloomingdale's. He was given the "best shoe salesman of the year" award five times, which was amazing when you consider he was also fired from Neiman's, Nordstrom's, Macy's and Bloomingdale's, almost always for offending or embarrassing his customers. Though 42, his boyish good looks, charming manner and sweet disposition caused the ladies to unconsciously gravitate toward him: perhaps to mother him as well as buy from him. Still, he could not resist the zingers.

I walked into his showroom one day to chat and found him surrounded by shoe cartons lying all over the floor. He was sitting on a stool in front of what must have been a very fussy lady because it looked as though she had tried on and rejected a dozen pair of shoes. Frustrated beyond belief, Billy excused himself, went back into the storeroom, and emerged with a very long shoebox. He took a pump out of it that had a three-foot feather sticking straight up from the heel, and said to the woman, "Now, here's something that will tickle your fancy."

On another occasion Billy was helping a very beautiful young woman try on shoes. She was wearing a miniskirt, so that each time she lifted her leg to try on a shoe, he was given a glimpse of paradise. She smiled at him coquettishly, he winked back, and they understood without saying more that it was time to retire to one of the nearby dressing rooms. Once there, they tore off each other's clothes, but before Billy could embrace her, she stepped back and smeared copious amounts of K-Y Jelly all over her privates. He hesitated and then asked, "Can I borrow your strand of pearls?" She said, "Sure, but why?" He said, "I'm not going in there without chains."

Then there was the time he was fitting a woman who was quite long in the tooth. She kept flirting with him to his great annoyance. Finally, she asked breathlessly, "And where have you been all of my life, you darling boy?" He answered, "Let me put it this way. For the first 50 years, I didn't exist."

Years later, an old girlfriend of Billy's came in to buy some shoes. She was still a good friend, they talked frequently, and they often gave each other advice on matters of the heart. She lamented to Billy that she was in a new relationship with a great guy and they planned to have sex for the first time that night. Billy said, "So, what's the problem?" She answered, "I have an appointment with my gynecologist two days from now regarding a possible yeast infection, and he advised me not to have sex for 48 hours before the exam." Billy asked, "Do you have a dental appointment as well?"

Perhaps his most confusing "romantic" moment as a shoe salesman occurred when he misinterpreted a customer's sexual intent. He invited her into a nearby dressing room and pressed his terrible swift sword into her palm. She gasped, "How dare you! Get out!" He answered, "I will, but first you're going to have to let go."

Mae

Mae grew up in hardscrabble West Virginia, the fourth daughter of a lifelong coal miner. Before the church admitted her as a novitiate, she was terribly abused by men up until her late 30s. She finally hit bottom as a prostitute in New Orleans and decided she could simply take no more. She joined the church and over the next 15 years served as a missionary in some of the most remote places in the world. Still, her past was her past and the mission sisters loved to hear her saucy stories

She told about the time she was ministering to the aborigines in Australia. She knew her efforts to bring the heathen to the Lord would come a cropper if they could not understand English, so to start she concentrated on educating the best hunter. They strolled through the bush and she would point out various features to him, pronounce their English names, and he would repeat them. That way he learned, "Stream," "Kangaroo," and "Sunrise." On one occasion, they walked passed a couple making love behind a boulder and flustered, Mae cried out, "Riding a horse!" The hunter walked over to the lovers and buried his lance between the man's shoulders. Mae exclaimed, "Why did you do that?" and he calmly replied, "That my horse."

Mae had been married two times before she found God, and was often asked by her co-workers, all virgins, what sex would be like if they had husbands. She said first comes "everywhere" sex where you make love in the living room, the attic, the basement, the breakfast nook, the dining room: basically, wherever there was a flat surface. Then there is "normal" sex where you make love in the master bedroom one or two nights a week after the children go to bed and the dog is let out. Lastly, there is "solo" sex where you walk past each other and growl, "Go fuck yourself!"

Mae related that she divorced her first husband because he was a drunkard and her second husband because of something she over-heard. She was cleaning up in the kitchen after a dinner party and could hear her husband through the kitchen door trying to calm a mortified young man who, sitting across from a buxom blonde, had said, "Those are some tits!" when he meant to say, "Those are some pits!" after two dessert peaches were cut in half. Mae's husband said, "You know, we all have slipups like that. It's no big deal. Just the other day I meant to say to my wife, 'I'd like some more coffee,' but it came out, 'You really fucked me to a fare-thee-well, you goddamn bitch!'"

Mae could not emphasize enough the importance of caring for the aged and infirm, and keeping their spirits up with humor. At her sec-ond ministry she made a point of playing pinochle every day with the same group of old men even though hands trembled, mem-ories slipped and eyesight faded. They noticed a new, wrinkled, grey-haired patient shuffling around and asked Mae, "What's his story? He doesn't look too bad." Mae said, "When he was a child he was told that if he wanted to remain healthy he should make love up to five times a day, and apparently he's been doing that ever since." They asked, "How old is he?" She responded, "22."

Calvin

CALVIN WAS THE QUINTESSENTIAL "PROMISING athlete who went nowhere": The fastest runner in grade school, a track and basketball wonder in high school, and an all-American fullback in college. Sadly, the pros would not take him and he began that slow, inevitable downward spiral into sports mediocrity. He sorely missed the eager cheerleaders, the fawning alumni and the breathless newspaper coverage and now, in his forties, he was just an embittered, sarcastic, high school gym coach who could not resist gulling the credulous.

One day a dimwitted farm boy came into his office seeking personal advice. He played on the basketball team and when showering could not help but notice the well-endowed packages of the black athletes. He wistfully wished he could be like that and asked, "Coach, is there any way I can get bigger?" Calvin replied, "Yeah. Tie a brick to your penis and let it hang down for two weeks and that should do it." Two weeks later the farm boy came back to Calvin's office with a big grin on his face. Calvin asked, "How'd it go?" The farm boy gushed, "Well, it's not any bigger, but it is turning black!"

At one of the commencement ceremonies, Calvin was asked to give a motivational speech to the graduates. He was still regarded by many as a hero who brought glory, however fleeting, to their small town. The principal asked him to emphasize the importance of obtaining a practical degree rather than something more esoteric but less remunerative. Calvin addressed the graduates, and said, "With a physics degree you can ask: 'What laws of nature are behind that?' With an engineering degree you can ask, 'What makes it work?' With a finance degree you can ask, 'How do you monetize that?' And with a liberal arts degree, you can ask, 'You want a coke with that?'"

The school's top athlete, a moron, came in one day to tell Calvin he could not play football that night because he was injured. Calvin could see that both his ears were covered in bandages. He asked, "How did that happen?" The athlete replied, "I was making tea for my Mom last night when the phone rang and, without looking, I picked up the hot kettle and pressed it to my ear." Calvin said, "Wow, that must gave hurt! But why is your other ear bandaged?" The athlete replied: "I had to call an ambulance, didn't I?"

Calvin told me he really hated one of the other gym teachers and obsessed about what he could do to drive him nuts. Then, he hit upon a brilliant idea. He bribed the teacher's housemaid to steal his remote control and now, when the mood strikes him, he drives back and forth near the teacher's house and turns the TV on and off.

Calvin also comforts lousy athletes with this story of a personal setback: "When I was down and out and a drunk, I shuffled into a church one day and asked God, 'Why have you done this to me? I'm broke, homeless, on drugs, and a total wreck.' A shaft of light pierced the gloom and a halo formed around me and a thunderous voice said, 'Because you *pissed* me off!'"

Ephraim

EPHRAIM WAS AN ISRAELI COMMANDO before he relocated to the United States at 26. He settled into life as a security consultant and with his good looks and affable personality traveled around the country making friends, charming members of the opposite sex, and closing one deal after another. He saw no need to mention that he was given early discharge from the Israeli Defense Force for being both insubordinate and a wise ass, but his war stories were always a delight to his clients.

He told of the misery of his basic training and how he was assigned to a platoon leader who rode him unmercifully for almost all of it. But before he finished his training, the platoon leader retired and at his going away party said to Ephraim, "I'm guessing after I die you'll come and piss on my grave." Ephraim sipped his beer and replied, "No. I'm through standing in lines."

For a while Ephraim trained as a medic but washed out of that specialty when a complaint for molestation was filed against him. He told me it was a misunderstanding and what really happened was that he was examining a female jet fighter pilot who was damn pretty and coming on to him, so he thought she might enjoy "playing doctor." He stroked her thigh and said, "Just checking for abrasions." She smiled. He fondled her breasts and said, "Just looking for calcification." She smiled again. Emboldened, he stoked her vagina and said, "Just checking for genital warts" and she groaned lasciviously. Thus encouraged, he dropped his pants, entered her, and said, "Can you guess what I'm doing now?" She said, "Catching crabs?"

Ephraim's commando squad was given the mission of securing a small, uninhabited island off the Syrian coast that the IDF wanted to use as a listening post. Ephraim went ashore first to scout out the island and to his astonishment stumbled on a small town that was perfect in every way. It had homes and stores and fences and gardens, and sitting in its park was a small, swarthy man who waved him over. He joined the man and asked, "What's your name? Why are you here?" The man said his name was Saul Greenberger, he got stranded on the island 30 years ago, he built the town himself, and it even had two synagogues. Ephraim asked, "Why is that?" Saul responded, "Every Jew needs a temple he wouldn't be caught dead in."

Another time while on leave, Ephraim attended a Quaker meeting in Pennsylvania. As the leader called on various members by name to stand and say something helpful to others, Ephraim realized the meeting had many Goldsteins, Werners, and Schwartzes so at the conclusion of the meeting he asked the leader why that was and the leader said, "It's no big deal. Some of my best Jews are Friends."

Finally, when meeting Muslims, Ephraim likes to point to the sky and say: "Let's kill each other in a religious war to see who has a better invisible friend up there."

Peter

PETER WAS A DISILLUSIONED CAPTAIN of industry. His rise through the corporate ranks was meteoric; so meteoric, in fact, that he was burned out at 50 and turned to religion and philosophy for meaning. One night, on his 65th birthday, over a few drinks in a friendly bar, he told me about his 15-year quest for enlightenment and some of the things that happened to him.

He recently returned home a broken man. He said he had heard of a guru in the Himalayas who knew the meaning of life and decided to go in search of him. For three years he trekked in the mountains through scorching suns and fierce blizzards, and it cost him his family, his fortune and his health. After his last two Sherpas perished in an avalanche, and he was ready to collapse and die, he stumbled into a small cave that grew bigger as he explored deeper. He finally entered a mammoth cavern with blazing torches and a little old monk sitting high up on a stone parapet. He fell to his knees and cried, "Oh, great Guru, I have sacrificed everything to come here and ask you one question." The Guru said, "Yes, my son." Peter gasped, "Can you tell me the meaning of life?" The Guru thought a for moment and said, "Life is just a bowl of cherries." Peter exploded, "What? After all I've been through, you tell me life is just a bowl of cherries!" Puzzled, the Guru leaned forward and said, "You mean life isn't just a bowl of cherries?"

Before his trek in the mountains, Peter lived in a monastery with a group of Benedictine monks and took a vow of silence. However, it was the practice of the order to allow one monk to speak a few words each year. The first year a monk said, "The soup is always too cold." The next year, another monk said, "I don't think the soup is too cold." The third year it was Peter's turn and he said, "I'm getting out of here. Your endless arguing is driving me nuts."

Because he was so immersed in religious thought, Peter often dreamed he was having a conversation with God. On many an occasion he was humbled by concepts so far beyond his comprehension he could only marvel at God's vision of time and space. In one conversation, he asked God, "How fast does a billion years pass for you?" God replied, "Just one second." Peter then asked, "What is a billion dollars worth to you?" God replied, "Just one dime." Peter then asked, "Can I have a dime?" God replied, "Just one second."

On another occasion, Peter dreamed he had passed away and that the meaning of life would at last be revealed to him. He arrived at the pearly gates but was denied entrance on the grounds he was not yet dead. Desperate for revelation, he tried every argument he could think of to convince St. Peter he had shuffled off his mortal coil. St. Peter finally said, "Are you willing to test it?" Peter thought about it and warily agreed, but with great trepidation. So, St. Peter said, "Do you believe dead men can breathe?" Peter responded, "No, of course not." Whereupon, he was punched in the stomach and gasping for breath gulped, "I'll be damned. Dead men *can* breathe."

Stella

"STELLA THE NUN!" THAT'S WHAT her girlfriends called her in eighth grade because she was so pure, so kind, so sweet and so understanding. In college, the frat boys recommended she join a convent because she was so chaste, so innocent, so pristine and so stubborn. When she actually did became a nun at 25, her family was amazed because she was so beautiful, so promising, so smart and so freedom-loving. On reflection, however, they agreed that those were the very traits that would make her a good nun.

Her innocence became evident when she and another nun were passing two rabbis in the street. It happened the rabbis had just come from Pincus The Tailor's where they picked up two suits they had ordered to be as black as possible. As they walked toward the nuns, they could see the nuns' habits were far blacker than their suits. After the rabbis passed by, Stella said to the other nun, "Wasn't it wonderful how that man spoke Latin?" The nun asked, "What did he say?" Stella chirped, "Pincus Fuctus!"

With a twinkle in her eye, Stella told me about a fantasy of hers where God comes to her and gives her permission to ask three questions. She asks, "Will I ever be able to marry?" God answers, "Not during your time on earth." She then asks, "Will I ever be able to become a priest?" God answers, "Not during your time on earth." Finally she asks, "Will there ever be a woman Pope?" God answers "Not during my time in heaven."

She also told me about the time she was walking with a group of nuns toward the convent when a dry-cleaning truck pulled alongside and the driver asked, "Do you have any filthy habits?"

Her sense of humor became evident when she recounted her conversation with a parish priest in which she admitted taking the Lord's name in vain while playing golf with other nuns. He asked, "Because you hooked the drive?" She answered, "No." "Because you topped the fairway iron?" "Not really." "Because you shanked the wedge?" "Heavens no!" "Because the wedge left you 30 feet from the hole?" "Gosh, no. I landed five inches from the pin." "Did you take the Lord's name in vain then?" "Certainly not." "Jesus Christ! You missed a five-inch putt?"

She also loved to pose riddles. She once asked me, " What do you get when a Jehovah's Witness marries an atheist and they have a baby?" I asked, "What?" She giggled, "A child who rings doorbells but doesn't know why." I groaned. So, she asked, "What church do the offspring of Jewish–Catholic marriages go to?" I asked, "What?" She smiled, "The Church Of Our Lady Of Perpetual Guilt."

She also tried to help a fallen nun who was having an affair with a dentist and used her patient visits to leave the convent. Stella warned, "The Mother Superior will find out." The nun said, "She suspects nothing." Stella said, "But you only have two teeth left."

Part 6

Della

DELLA WAS WASHINGTON'S "HOSTESS WITH the mostest." Politicians, diplomats, cabinet members, and general officers vied for her attention and clamored to be invited to her lavish parties. Deals were made, careers advanced, liaisons confirmed, and conspiracies consummated in the extravagant setting of her spectacular mansion in nearby Silver Spring, Maryland. She was the 60-year-old widow of a Jewish copper magnate and dedicated her life and fortune to be a mover and shaker in the only way she knew how: with consummate good taste and wicked wit.

For a short while after Della became a widow, she seriously contemplated marrying someone who would compliment her lifestyle: someone who had attained prominence through great achievement. But she could not get past the possibility such a man would only be after her money. She finally decided to remain a widow after showing the door to a likely candidate, causing me to inquire, "What went wrong?" She said, "When I asked him if he had fallen in love with me because my husband left me a fortune, he replied,

'Certainly not! I would love you regardless of who left you the fortune.'"

The honoree at one of her parties was a world-famous archaeologist who had made a stunning discovery of a mummy buried for thousands of years near the Dead Sea. What amazed everyone was the archaeologist's claim that, based on a sheet of papyrus found in the mummy's casket, he died of a heart attack. Stella's girlfriend asked her, "How could he tell the mummy had a heart attack?" Stella replied, "The papyrus said, 'Bet it all on Goliath.'"

From time to time Stella would allow her mansion to be used for the weddings of good friends. Sadly, one woman she loved was damn near a nymphomaniac and Stella tried everything she could think of to cool her ardor. When I asked Stella if holding the wedding at her house would embarrass her, she said, "No, because I just discovered a cuisine that will reduce a women's sexual cravings by 85%." I asked, "What is it?" She said, "Wedding cake."

Shortly after that, Stella had to confront the possibility of a wedding at her mansion that she thought would bring nothing but trouble. Her son returned home from college and announced he had fallen in love with a Cherokee Indian and hoped they could be married at home. Stella warned him that a marriage of a Jewish boy to a Cherokee Indian could prove disastrous: especially because her parents would be unhappy with his religion. He insisted they loved him and had even given him an Indian name. When I visited Stella and she told me about the wedding, I asked, "What name did they give him?" Stella replied, "Sitting Shiva!"

Her most embarrassing moment occurred when a pretty woman in a very tight dress had trouble climbing her stairs. She reached back again and again trying to loosen her lower zipper, but only succeeded in opening a delighted stranger's fly four times.

Amal

AMAL IS A GENERAL PRACTITIONER. And he is a Sikh. And he wears a turban. He was born in Punjab, India and attended the Maulana Azad Medical College in New Delhi. A shortage of doctors in HMOs around the U.S. created an opportunity for him to come to America. His employer paid for his family to move to St. Louis, provided offices and patients for him to attend and, best of all, provided malpractice insurance for free. Though his full beard and turban project a certain fierceness, he is a pussycat at heart and is endlessly amused by some of the health concerns of American patients and the observations he wished he could have made about them.

One patient did not trust his diagnosis and demanded a second opinion. Amal thought, "All right. You're stupid."

Another said she had an orgasm every time she sneezed and wanted it to stop. Amal was afraid that if he asked what she took for it, she would say, "Pepper."

An older man said he felt like vomiting whenever he looked in the mirror. Amal refrained from saying, "You've 20-20 eyesight."

An even older man said that every time he raised his arm it hurt and wanted to know what he could do about it. Amal started to say, "Don't raise your arm," but demurred.

Amal had a patient he disliked intensely because the man was both hateful and discourteous toward his religion. He used to fantasize he told the man, "I'm afraid I have bad news for you and even worse news for you." The man asked, "What's the bad news?" Amal said, "Unfortunately, you've only got a week to live." Stunned, the man asked, "What's worse than that?" Amal smiled, "I tried calling you last week."

He was not always a general practitioner. Before he left India, Amal was a surgeon, but even there he had to hold his tongue. He was about to operate on a young prostitute who asked him how long it would be before she could resume sexual activities, and he caught himself before saying, "I've never had a patient ask that before a tonsillectomy!"

Amal also told me about a patient he was examining who could not stop talking about a newspaper that printed his obituary even though he was very much alive. Worse yet, no one from the paper had returned his calls. He asked Amal if that happened often in India and Amal said it did, but the Indian newspapers had worked out a standard response if a caller got through. The patient asked, "What was it?" And try as he might, Amal could not resist saying, "Where are you calling from?"

His saddest and most surprising consultation was with a woman who was having severe heart problems. He had no need to hold his tongue. He said honestly, "You should know, you have acute angina." She blushed and said, "Do you really think so?"

Bruce

BRUCE IS A HAIRDRESSER. HE wished his name was Margaret. He suspected his sexual preferences at 10 and was certain of them at 16 when he fell hopelessly in love with a fullback. Now, at 30, he is effeminate to the core. Fashion models mimic his walk and hand gestures. Jewelry manufacturers seek his advice on necklaces, bracelets and brooches. His bangs are *de rigueur* in women's magazines. And his lovers are legion. Emotional as he is, sarcasm keeps bubbling to the surface.

Bruce was quite free with his advice. You might say he was an unrestrained busybody. He told me he annoyed one particular customer by repeatedly criticizing her decisions, but she got back at him in the end. If she bought a condo in Manhattan, Bruce said she should have bought a beach house in the Hamptons. If she bought a Mercedes, Bruce said she should have bought a Rolls Royce. If she said she was going to the inauguration, Bruce said she should go to the inaugural ball instead. After the inauguration, she said she met the President. Bruce asked, "Did you speak to him?" She replied, "Yes, he made a comment as he passed by." Bruce asked,

"What was it?" She said, "Jesus Christ, who gave you that shitty haircut!"

A bald customer came in and said he tried emollients, a wig and a hair transplant but they either did not work, or looked ridiculous, or hurt way too much. The customer had always admired the fullness and silkiness of Bruce's hair and said, "Make my head look like yours and it's worth $10,000 to me." So Bruce shaved his head.

Bruce offered to sell a wide range of cosmetics to a particularly vain customer who said she wanted to look younger. She spent hours applying the creams and lotions and then went to see Bruce for his professional opinion. She asked, "Do I look younger?" He said, "From your eyes, 24; from your complexion, 17; from your body, 25." She blushed, "How flattering." He said, "Hold a sec, I need to add them up."

Another incredibly vain customer came in and asked Bruce, "Can you make me look like the girl next door?" Bruce answered, "Sure, if you live next to a junkyard."

One of Bruce's customers was a closet homosexual. His doctor, who knew his patient was gay, and who also knew Bruce was gay, gave him Viagra to facilitate sex with his wife and save their marriage. The customer told Bruce he had taken the Viagra a few days ago in anticipation of his wife coming home, but she called to say she would be delayed several hours. In desperation, he called the doctor and said, "What am I going to do with this tremendous hard on? My wife won't be home for hours!" The doctor said, "Can Bruce help?" The customer exclaimed, "I don't need Viagra with Bruce!"

Bruce also told me they developed a new pill for gays that combined Spanish fly with tranquilizer and it was called "Span-Tran." He said, 'It gets you hot as hell, but if you don't get anywhere, you don't give a damn."

Lee

LEE WAS A LONG-HAUL TRUCK driver. You would expect him to be a big, burly guy with a beer belly and tattoos when in fact he could easily be taken for the friendly neighborhood milkman who, in the old days, delivered bottled milk and dairy products door-to-door. Being skinny, short, near-sighted, and hard-of-hearing in no way disqualified him from driving the very biggest rigs. And although he majored in philosophy in college, he could not resist the call of the open road and brought a worldly-wise perspective to the job.

He told me of the time he was sitting on a wooden bench at a truck stop having his lunch when three Hell's Angels roared into the parking lot. They were mean and looking for trouble. They walked over to him and the first one spit in his sandwich, the second one poured his soda on the ground, and the third one ate his dessert. Without objecting, Lee got into his truck and drove away. I asked him, "Didn't you want to fight back?" He said, "Why? I backed over their Harleys."

Last year Lee was driving along the Texas-Mexico border and noticed a small lake of oil aflame in a field so he called it in. Within half an hour a truck full of Mexicans with serapes and sombreros drove to a hill above the fire and, after hesitating for a few moments, drove right down into the middle of it and beat it out with their sombreros. Lee was nearby when the rig owner paid the boss of the Mexicans $10,000. Lee congratulated the boss on his team's skill and courage and asked if they were going to party with the money. The boss replied, "No, Senor. Thees time I get brakes on fucking truck feexd."

Lee had partied with the guys one night and was blotto when a rookie cop stopped his weaving rig and began to write a ticket. He asked Lee, "What have you been drinking?" Feeling frisky, Lee said, "I started the night with a six-pack of beer. After that, I drank tequila shooters with the guys. Then, a sweet honey had me join her for a few scotch and sodas, and I finished the night with five rum and cokes." The cop said, "You're going to have to take a Breathalyzer test." Lee said, "Why? You think I'm lying?"

Lee knows he is too drunk to drive when he puts both contact lenses in the same eye.

He picked up a rather gullible hitchhiker heading east after visiting California for the first time, and the hitchhiker could not stop talking about what a strange place it was. He said there were towns there whose names were spelled completely differently from the way they were pronounced. Lee said, "I know. They have a town there spelled L-a J-o-l-l-a, and they pronounce it 'San Luis Obispo.'"

On a number of occasions, Lee carried livestock in Oklahoma. He asked me, "Do you know the difference between a sheep farmer and a sheep herder?" I said, "No, what?" He said, "The farmer raises sheep and the herder gets emotionally involved."

Woody

WOODY IS AN EXTERMINATOR. HE used to spray insecticide in orchid hothouses, but gave that up when his skin turned green. Then he got a pilot's license and became a crop duster, but pancaked into the ground once too often. He also tried termite tenting and mold removal, but finally settled on being an exterminator so he could battle the enemy one-on-one in a field of his choosing. In his HAZMAT suit with a tank strapped to his back he looked the proper spaceman, but inside the suit he was just a good-looking 34-year-old with a smile that could kill and an attitude that could use adjusting.

The first time I met Woody he told me that time is fun when you're having flies.

He also told me not to be surprised, when looking for ants with a magnifying glass on a sunny day, at how readily they ignite.

Woody was treating some baseboards in a hotel room when he overheard a husband and wife having a conversation in the room next door. The husband asked, "Why don't you tell me I have a great body anymore?" "Because," she replied, "you don't have a great body anymore." He then asked, "Well, why don't you tell me I'm a loving husband anymore?" Because," she said, "you're not loving husband anymore." He then asked, "Well, why don't you tell me when you have a great orgasm anymore?" She said, "I don't know where to reach you."

At another hotel job, Woody was waiting in the lobby for his partner before going upstairs when he overheard an elderly lady with a southern accent scorching a bellhop. She complained, "What is this? This room's ridiculously tiny. There's no furniture, no ventilation, not even a bed. What do you think I am, some dumb cracker?" The bellhop patiently explained, "It's the elevator, Ma'am."

Woody was also doing some work sanitizing the doctor's lounge at a local hospital when two surgeons came in arguing about who were the best patients to operate on. The first surgeon said, "I like to operate on Germans the best because when you cut them open, everything is in order." The second surgeon said, "I like to operate on Japanese the best because when you cut them open, everything is color-coded." They noticed Woody sweeping up some debris and out of curiosity asked him whom he would like to operate on best if he were a surgeon. Without hesitation, he answered, "Lawyers." One of the surgeons asked "Why?" and Woody said, "Because when you cut them open, you find no brains, no guts, and the mouth and asshole are interchangeable."

A homeowner once asked Woody to treat an infestation of bird droppings on his home's back deck. He had a wooden leg, a hook and an eye patch and explained he had been a fisherman, fell overboard, and lost his leg and his hand to sharks. Woody asked, "What about the eye?" He said, "Oh, that. A pigeon crapped in my eye and I tried to wipe it away with my finger. Unfortunately, it was only my second day with the hook."

Geoff

GEOFF IS A CERTIFIED PUBLIC Accountant: a "CPA." To those unfriendly towards him, he is a Certified Public Asshole. He makes absolutely no effort to get along with his co-workers at the firm. Yet his obsequiousness toward and ass-kissing of clients are legendary and embarrassing to watch. But he has the tenacity of a bulldog so the partners give him the toughest assignments and know he will get to the bottom of the books. Since he is now 15 years out of college, he has high hopes of a partnership and with each year's delay he becomes grumpier and grumpier.

I was able to measure the man when, with a smirk on his face, he told me some of his favorite accountant jokes: First, he asked me, "Did you hear about the constipated accountant?" When I said, "No," he said, "He worked it out with a pencil." I groaned. Then, he asked me, "What does a gay accountant say to a good-looking man at the bar of a gay saloon?" When I asked, "What?" he said, "May I push in your stool?" Oh, my, oh, my. Lastly, he asked me, "What do accountants do to make their Christmas parties more exciting?"

I said, "Tell me," and he said, "Send invitations to funeral directors." Okay, a bit better.

He was once auditing a client who was told she had only seven months to live. I asked him if he treated her with more respect after he learned the bad news. He said, "Most definitely, I urged her to marry an accountant right away, and she asked, 'Will that allow me to live longer?' I said, 'No, but it will be the longest seven months of your life.'"

He also said he had a client who received a very hard lesson in long division. Apparently, he decided to leave his wife and attached a photo of himself and his young girlfriend on the beach in Barbados to a text that read, "How's that for a 60-year-old man and a 19-year-old fox?" Two days later he received a photo from his wife and her 19-year-old lover cavorting at a pool in St. Bart's. It was attached to a text that read, "How's that for a 60-year-old woman and a 19-year-old Adonis? And remember, 19 goes into 60 a lot more than 60 goes into 19."

Because Geoff worked so hard and so long to prove he was partnership material, his wife was unhappy with the small amount of time he spent with their five-year-old son, Billy. She constantly badgered Geoff to bond with the boy and to do father-son activities that would be of interest to his son. Finally, Geoff and Billy went on a "guys" outing and when they got home, Geoff's wife asked Billy if he had fun? He answered, "Yes, Daddy took me to a big animal park and one of them paid 20-to-1."

Geoff also told me he was recently forced to make an urgent call to his insurance broker and said, "I need to buy a casualty policy on my house right away. Can I do it while we're talking?" The broker said, "No, an on-site inspection is necessary." Geoff said, "Well, could you please come over right away. The broker said, "We usually need 24-hours notice in advance to do an inspection. What's the hurry?" Geoff said, "It's ablaze."

Chatan

CHATAN IS A 45-YEAR-OLD SIOUX Indian. His name stands for "Hawk." The Sioux also call themselves Lakota or Dakota or Nakota. Chatan lives on the reservation, serves on the tribal council, and follows the old ways. Although he received a finance degree in college that qualifies him to keep the books and handle the important correspondence of the tribe, he thinks it imperative that its members continue to observe their cultural and ceremonial customs such as the sweat lodge, the sun dance, and the healing ceremony. Because he stands at the crossroads of the new and old, his attitude is one of bemused paternalism.

He once tended the ""Soothsayer" booth at a county fair organized by his tribe. His shtick was that he could tell where people hailed from just by looking at their clothing. If he were wrong he would give them a bracelet with a turquoise centerpiece. Three cowboys approached his booth and challenged his skill. He successfully guessed the first cowboy was from Colorado because of the style of his Stetson. He successfully guessed the second cowboy was from Idaho because of his Bullhide hat. Before he could get to the third cowboy, the cowboy ripped off his hat and hid it. Chatan looked at him a moment and said, "You're from Mississippi." The startled cowboy said, "How could ya tell. I ain't wearin' no hat?" Chatan replied, "Your pants are on backwards."

Chatan was quite naïve when he married his sweet little squaw. As they were driving east toward Rapid City for their honeymoon, he stroked her thigh and she breathed heavily, "Please go farther than that," so he drove her to Sioux Falls.

He also worked at a cowboy bar off the reservation in his youth and told me this story while chuckling: He said that a city slicker walked into the bar dressed in a three-piece suit and a cowboy asked him where he was from and what line of work he was in. He said, "I'm from Atlanta and I specialize in taxidermy. I mount dead animals." The cowboy jumped up and shouted to the other wranglers, "Stand down, boys. He's family!"

On one of my visits to the bar, Chatan told me about a bragging fight he had earlier in the day with an inebriated Texas cattle baron. The Texan asked him the size of his reservation and Chatan said it was about 3,469 square miles. The Texan said, "That's nothin'. With my car, I can drive from mornin' to night and never cross all my land." Chatan observed, "I had a car like that, too."

Lastly, an Okie from Muskogee came into the bar and ordered eight shots of bourbon, one right after the other. Chatan asked, "Are you celebrating something?" The Okie said proudly, "I was on the reservation doing an audit for the Bureau Of Indian Affairs to see if further natural resource management services were needed, and I stumbled into a party at the Tribal Council headquarters. I got lucky and had the first blow job of my life." Chatan said, "Congratulations! Can I offer you another shot of bourbon on the house?" The Okie said, "Nah, if I couldn't get rid of the taste with eight, a ninth won't help."

Rhoda

WHEN THINGS ARE NOT GOING smoothly, when operations are chaotic, when production lines slow down, they call for Rhoda. She is the 60-year-old founder of one of the leading "efficiency expert" firms in the nation. She received a B.A. in industrial engineering, an M.B.A in business, and a Ph.D. in marketing, and earned her chops with multi-year careers at Boeing, United Technologies, and General Motors. Being of steel mind and stout body, her competitors call her "smart like bull; strong like fox."

Rhoda told me about her significant other, Filbert, who agreed to a division of labor in their domestic unit whereby she would be the breadwinner and he would be the homemaker. She loved him dearly but could not abide his inefficiency and, sadly, her efforts to reform him backfired. When he made and served dinner he would go back and forth to the kitchen carrying one item only, and Rhoda urged him to carry several items at once to save time. She muttered ruefully, "It actually worked. When it used to take him an hour to serve dinner, it only takes me 15 minutes."

She also encouraged Filbert to multitask while driving in order to speed the completion of his chores, even though that advice was contrary to the recommendations of the Department of Motor Vehicles. She said he called her one very hectic day to give her good and bad news and she said, "Just give me the good news. I'm really busy." So, he piped up, "The air bag worked perfectly!"

Rhoda moved into new offices a year ago to be closer to some major clients. She was organizing her office when someone knocked on her door. Assuming it was one of her clients who decided to pay a welcome visit, and wanting to look both busy and professional, Rhoda picked up the phone and started to discuss time and motion studies with an imaginary client. She turned to the door and said, "Come in," and then continued with her conversation. A nice-looking young man in casual clothes walked in and she said to him, "May I help you?" and he said, "I'm here to turn on the phone."

When asked if spanking was efficient, Rhoda said, "Only for consenting adults."

Rhoda often gave seminars to physician groups seeking to streamline their practices. She liked to begin her speeches with a joke to lighten the mood and told me the one the doctors liked best: She would say to her audience, "Two of the doctors sitting together today, a man and a woman, had an interesting experience last night and we will offer a door prize to anyone who can identify them. They met at the 'Welcome' cocktail party and then went to dinner and she washed her hands both before and after the meal. Then, because they really hit it off, they went to his room to make love and she washed her hands both before and after sex. This morning he said to her, 'You're a surgeon, aren't you?' She asked, 'How could you tell?' He replied, 'By how frequently you wash your hands.' Then, she said, 'And you're an anesthetist, right?' He said, 'Yeah, how could you tell?' She replied, 'I didn't feel a thing last night.'"

Joe

JOE HAD THE LEGAL CAREER every lawyer dreams about: Princeton undergraduate, Harvard law, a clerkship with the Chief Justice of the Supreme Court of New Jersey, senior partner in the top firm in Newark, and a federal district court judgeship at 60. He also had a skewed sense of humor. As we sat under a shade tree at his house in Princeton watching my kids and his grandkids frolic in the pool, and our wives staggering under a tray piled with steaks for the barbeque, I said, "Even though you took out huge loans for your education and struggled for years, when you see all this…?" And before I could finish the question he mused, "No, it wasn't worth it."

I was in his courtroom for the second week of a product liability class-action lawsuit having a potential outcome in the hundreds of millions of dollars. The case had taken two years to reach this point and the trial promised to last three months. Joe was very anxious to move the case along without interruption because his docket was badly overcrowded. He entered the courtroom and after every-one was seated was startled to see an empty seat in the jury box.

"Where's the missing juror?" he demanded of the foreman who replied, "Your Honor, the missing juror is a rabid football fan and he had to leave to attend the Super Bowl this weekend, but it's okay because he left his verdict with me."

The same day, Joe read the indictment concerning the theft of 20 television sets to a slow-witted man standing before him. He said, "You know you're the defendant, right?" The man protested, "Am not! I only stole the TVs."

Last year, Joe was the featured speaker at the Bar Association's annual meeting and opened with this: "Three men were adrift in a lifeboat after their cruise liner sank: a doctor, a lawyer and an architect. They paddled frantically toward a nearby island but the current was too strong and they knew they would miss it, so they drew straws to see who would swim through shark-infested waters to get help. The lawyer lost, jumped overboard, swam for it, and as he did so the sharks opened up a path for him. Later, around the campfire of the islanders who saved them, the doctor said to the lawyer, 'It was amazing how those sharks opened a path for you,' and the lawyer responded, 'Not really - just a matter of professional courtesy.'"

When Joe was in London visiting Westminster Abbey, the guide pointed to a slab on the floor and said, "Buried there is an ethical man and a great lawyer." Puzzled, Joe asked, "You put two men in the same crypt?"

Finally, Joe could not resist giving this advice at law school graduation ceremonies: "First, if the law is against you, argue the facts. If the facts are against you, argue the law. If they're both against you, insult the judge. Second, it doesn't matter whether you're right or wrong as long as you sound authoritative. Third, let your law firm's motto be, 'Seldom right, but never in doubt.' Fourth, let's turn to more serious matters…"

Eric

WHEN OTHER KIDS PLAYED BASEBALL or computer games or tag, Eric was off shooting photos with a pretend camera. In high school he preferred the point and shoot. In college he liked the compacts. In the army he used only a digital single reflex. And now, news photography being his profession, he uses a Hasselblad H5D-200c Multi-Shot Medium Format DLRS camera which set him back a cool $44,955. Its images are as sharp as his mind and its accuracy as crisp as his guile.

One of his first assignments was covering the White House for The San Francisco Chronicle. He told me there were endless hours of boredom waiting for the president to make news. There were so many celebrities passing through that he and his colleagues often debated the meaning of "being important" and knowing when you have reached that status. One photographer opined, "You know you're important when you are invited to a state dinner." Another opined "You know you're important when you are chatting with the president in the Oval Office and he refuses to take other calls." Eric opined, "You know you're important when the hotline to Moscow rings, the president picks it up, listens, and says, 'It's for you.'"

Eric often covered crime scenes and at one of them took photos of a suspect who was arrested in the vicinity. He followed up with some shots of the "perp" in jail and confided to him, "I heard your blood tests came back and there's both bad and good news. The bad news is that your DNA was found on the victim's body. The good news is your triglycerides are below 150."

The caption he chose for one of his photos was, "Man Denies He Died in Toledo!"

He also told me of an unusual event that allegedly occurred when he was photographing some baby animals at the zoo. A woman with a tight sweater was agitating the silverback and her husband urged Eric to shoot his wife sideways with the gorilla shaking his cage in the background. Then he urged him to shoot his wife topless with the gorilla jumping up and down in the background. Then he urged him to shoot his wife naked with the gorilla thumping his chest in the background. Then he threw his wife into the cage and snarled; "Now try telling him you're too tired!"

I accompanied Eric when his assignment was to photograph the wedding of a famous politician's daughter. As the bride came down the aisle, I mused aloud, "I wonder why wedding dresses are always white?" Eric answered, "Kitchen equipment is always white."

I also accompanied him when he was covering the Masters Tournament. We got lucky and were invited to play between professional rounds by the chairman of the Augusta National Golf Club. I was doing terribly and asked Eric what was wrong with my game. He said, "I think you stand too close to the ball after you strike it."

Part 7

Red

RED STUDIED AT THE SORBONNE and visited all the obligatory art centers in Europe. You would often find him at museums copying the paintings of the masters. He began his career at 20 as a bright, optimistic, and enthusiastic portrait artist but as lack of success dogged his efforts, he also experimented with abstract expressionism, surrealism, minimalism, cubism and finally pop art. Now, he is a relatively bitter and disillusioned 40-year-old house painter who has at least kept his sense of humor and sketches abstract masterpieces on house walls before painting over them. We often enjoy drinks after work when he tells me about the quirky things he sees or hears during the day.

Very early one morning, Red arrived at the home of the father of the bride who was expecting the newlyweds home around noon. He asked Red to quickly finish painting the rooms they would be living in. They didn't show up when expected and the father asked the family, "Has anyone seen them?" The bride's little sister piped up, "I did! They came in late last night and stayed in the guest room. Bill came out for looking for something called 'K-Y Jelly' but I couldn't find it so I gave him my dolls' super glue."

On another occasion, Red was painting the luxury home of a very successful investment banker who had been caught having an affair by his wife. He overheard their conversation in the living room. She was obviously in distress and spoke very softly. He was scrambling as fast he could. He said to her, "Sweetheart, I'm so sorry. Please let me show you how much I love you. What would you like? A private jet? A yacht? A second home in Aspen? Please tell me what you want." She said quietly, "A divorce." He said, "Shit, I hadn't planned on spending that much."

Red was asked to paint a room on the sixth floor of a hotel on an emergency basis. He hit it off with one of the chambermaids and at the end of the day they went to the room to make love. It was empty except for a throw rug on the floor. As they were going at it, she complained there was a projection under the rug hurting her back. Red looked under the rug, saw a steel plate, and removed it with a screwdriver. Later, as he left the hotel, he saw police cars and an ambulance outside the lobby. He asked a bellhop, "What happened?" The bellhop answered, "Some guy on the fifth floor was hit by a chandelier."

Last year, Red wound up painting the entire floor of an office building because of positive referrals from one customer to another. As he was painting around an air duct in the ceiling of one office, he overheard a conversation in a sex therapist's office on the floor above. The wife complained, "There is just so little passion in our marriage." The therapist said, "Perhaps you could wear a saucy negligee." She replied, "I did. He was indifferent." He suggested,

"Perhaps beautiful music would enhance the mood." She said, "I tried. He yawned." He advised, "Perhaps you could look deeply into his eyes while making love." She said, "I tried once. It was awful. He was furious." He asked, "Why so?" She said, "He was looking at me through the bedroom window."

Deirdre

DEIRDRE IS AN IRISH BABY'S name, and was the name of a tragic character in Irish legend who died of a broken heart. Our Deidre is a real
estate broker who is tough as nails, and the only thing that makes
her cry is a lost commission. She is competitive beyond measure:
whether completing Girl Scout projects first, scoring more soccer
goals than her high school teammates, or stealing boyfriends from
her college sorority sisters. She was named "Best Broker Of The
Year" five times and earned the most commissions in her firm seven
years running. You would think at 55 she would slow down, but
"closing the deal" is still her greatest passion.

In her last deal, she was selling a house to an incredibly naïve couple
and, taking pity on them, decided just this once to be completely
candid about its features rather than shading the truth to make a
sale. She said, "This house is bordered on the south by a chemical
waste plant, on the east by a paper factory, on the north by an oil
refinery, and on the west by a slaughterhouse. The husband sputtered, "Jesus Christ! Is there nothing good you can say about this

house?" Deidre conceded, "Well, it's easy to tell which way the wind is blowing."

Deirdre told me she had to testify in an acrimonious divorce proceeding where the parties were arguing over how to split the value of their luxury penthouse. She was called as an expert witness to assess the property but was also encouraged by the attorneys to assign fault to one party or the other since the case involved infidelity. She testified, "Well, the husband was an international banker who traveled a great deal during the week, and told me he came home from a trip one Saturday night and made mad, passionate, noisy love to his wife until some guy in the adjoining penthouse pounded on the wall and screamed, 'Can you at least not fuck on the weekend?'"

After drinking heavily in a bar one night, Deirdre slurred to me, "When I was in my teens, I used to think that money and prestige would make me happy...I was right." In the same spirit, I confessed, "Since I was a kid I always wished I could be someone...but now I see I should have been more specific."

When she was just starting out, Deirdre was given a half share in a real estate brokerage owned by her uncle. He suggested, "Why don't you take a few extra courses in sales and marketing?" She declined, "I am so done with school." He said, "Okay, how about handling the open houses for the properties we have listed?" She demurred, "No, I'd be bored to death." He said, "Well, perhaps you could run the office and handle the paperwork." Sorry," she said, "I loathe clerical work." Frustrated, he snapped, "What the hell am I supposed to do with you?" She cooed, "How about buying me out?"

Deirdre's most enjoyable job interview was with a newly minted broker who demanded starting pay of $200,000. She said, "How about full benefits, first-class travel, five weeks vacation and a luxury car?" He said, "Are you kidding?" She said, "Aren't you?"

Tiffany

ONCE SHE DECIDED TO BE an actress in the movies, Tiffany had to decide if her persona for casting purposes would be that of ingénue, femme fatale, damsel in distress, or just plain starlet. Since she was a small star with a heavenly 22-year-old body, the appellation "starlet" stuck. She was also a fairly good actress so her hopes of becoming a star were not totally unrealistic; but only if she could overcome her somewhat-less-than-average intelligence and successfully manage producer lust. Please note I said, "manage," not "avoid."

To her embarrassment, Tiffany was identified as the adulteress in a suit for divorce brought by the wife of a producer she was seeing. She testified on the witness stand that she was not at fault because she was as much a victim of the producer's deceit as his wife. His attorney asked, "Why is that?" She said, "Well, when we went to the hotel in Las Vegas and registered, he told everyone I was his wife."

Tiffany tried very hard to fit in with Hollywood's elite and decided to hold a sophisticated dinner party for her then boyfriend, an established star. But she told me he broke her heart when, the day before the party, she sent him to a kiosk on the beach to buy high-quality lobsters, crabs, shrimp and snails and he stayed out all night. What woke her early the next morning was the sound of him dropping a bucket of snails on the stairs as he tiptoed to the kitchen. She flew out of the bedroom and demanded to know why he was out all night. He quickly turned to the snails sliming the stairs and said, "Let's go, boys, a few more steps and we're there."

Tiffany was also required to appear in an outdoor street scene in one of her early movies. Small crowds of people stood around watching the production. The director was getting exasperated with Tiffany because her acting was too soft and needed more grit. She looked for a way to convince the director she could be tough and, during a break in the shooting, went over to a group of people standing in line and demanded they move on, which they reluctantly did. She returned to the director and said, "How's that?" He said, "That was a bus stop."

When she turned 20, Tiffany accompanied a married producer to St. Croix. She had never been to the Caribbean before and felt she could put up with his boorish conduct in exchange for lots of sun, sand, gambling, and nightlife. She had sex with him twice before the trip and it was okay, not great. In bed their first night in St. Croix, she asked him, "What were you thinking before we first made love?" He answered, "I wanted to screw your brains out!" "And now that we're in the Caribbean?" "Obviously, I did."

The next night they went to a "cook your own" barbeque and the producer, fancying himself a gourmet, cooked some deer. Tiffany asked if it was veal or beef and he smirked, "Neither, it's what my wife calls me." She exclaimed, "We're having asshole?"

Steven

HE WANTED SO MUCH TO be pre-med but had to settle for a degree in biology. He wanted so much to go to medical school but even the second-rate universities in the Caribbean turned him down. He wanted so much to be a faith healer but no recognized church would accept him. He then tried to specialize in acupressure, acupuncture, hydrotherapy, aromatherapy, and homeopathy, but the alternative medical arts found him wanting. All this rejection stemmed from the simple fact that he was a blockhead and so, at 45, he found himself advocating birth control for the UN around the world.

I first met him in Tanzania when he served as an adjunct to the Peace Corps and told me that since the native women were hopeless in keeping count of birth control pills, he was demonstrating the use of condoms to the men. He said, "I may have not been as clear as I should have been. About three months after I started the training, a woman who had eight kids was pregnant again even though her husband had attended the first class. I asked her why he didn't keep the condom on and she said he did, but after a week he had to piss so bad he sliced the tip off."

In Poland he actually found himself on the other side of the issue. A distraught young woman who spoke only halting English came into his facility under the impression it was a fertility clinic and he was a gynecologist. Before he could straighten her out, she broke down into a spasm of weeping and confessed she could not get pregnant. He felt very sorry for her and wanting to help, but only in a harmless way, he said very slowly, "I take look and maybe fix. Take off panties and bend over table." She said, "I do it. But would rather have husband be father."

He then went to Hong Kong to learn a special technique they had for performing an abortion with almost no pain. They did it by re-distributing the pain from the mother to the father electronically in a way that allowed the gynecologist to reduce the wife's pain in one room and retransmit it to the father in another. The only thing uncertain was the range of the transmission. Steven monitored the husband during the procedure and kept reporting he was doing fine even though the gynecologist kept redirecting more and more of the wife's pain to him. None the worse for wear, the couple went home and found the gardener dead of a heart attack in the backyard.

Some newlyweds came to see Steven in Boston. After the session, Steven asked her, "How could you marry that ass?" She said, "Opposites attract. I was knocked up and he wasn't."

Steven also spent some time teaching birth control to farmers in hardscrabble Northern India where poverty compelled them to use and reuse everything they had. He gave demonstrations to the farmers on the mechanics of using condoms but emphasized the skins should be discarded immediately and not used again or for some other purpose. Two weeks after the class a frustrated wife told Steven he had to tell her husband to stop throwing the skins out the window because they were killing the chickens.

Paddy

PADDY WAS AN IRISH BARTENDER in Killarney. He was soft-spoken, easy to like, and always ready to listen. He was only 32 but his personality was so welcoming even senior citizens came to him with their complaints or seeking a sympathetic ear. He also dispensed advice freely and with the assurance of a sage. There was only one flaw: On occasion, and only on occasion, he would give advice or make a comment that ridiculed the speaker who was either so far gone or ridiculous in discourse he did not realize he had been had. I became friends with Paddy when I was on vacation in Ireland and he shared with me some of his better *bon mots* or *unintended gaffes*, as the case may be.

One day Paddy was talking to two drunks at the bar and asked them if they had heard about the tragedy that occurred at a nearby construction site. He told them three workers had thrown themselves off a sixth-story girder and left behind heartbroken and destitute wives. The drunks asked, "Why did they do it?" Paddy answered, "The Frenchman's wife kept making him pate sandwiches for lunch and he couldn't stand it any more so he checked out. The Greek did the same thing when all he got was hummus. But the Irishman was different. He committed suicide over corned beef." "Why was that different?" asked the drunks. Paddy smiled, "He made his own sandwiches."

Paddy told Grady, an unrepentant repeat offender, that if he was ever charged with rape and had to stand in a lineup, he should shout, "She's the one!" when the victim entered the room.

On another occasion, Paddy pretended to be an aggrieved husband when two inebriates were explaining why they thought their wives were having affairs. The first drunk said, "I think my wife is sleeping with a handyman because I found a screw driver under the bed." The second drunk said, "I think my wife is sleeping with a painter because I found a paint brush under the bed." Paddy said, "I think my wife is sleeping with a horse because I found a cowboy under the bed."

Paddy told a woozy customer that Paddy's neighbor, whom he loathed, moved away and forgot his backyard hose so he asked Paddy to mail it to him. Paddy smirked, "I did it in a box three inches wide, three inches high, and 60 feet long."

On another occasion, Paddy was chatting with an inebriated customer when the customer looked toward the front door and gasped, "Good God, my wife and my mistress just came in together!" Without batting an eye, Paddy said, "Me, too!"

Sometimes Paddy would pretend he once had a severe drinking problem in order to show camaraderie with a backsliding customer. He would say, "I used to visit a tavern where I was not liked very much, always ordered scotch and soda, often passed out drunk, and was often kicked in the balls. On my fifth visit, I ordered a gin and tonic. The bartender asked, 'Why the change?' and I told him, 'Scotch and soda hurts my balls.'"

Rebecca

REBECCA WAS NOT JUST A Jewish mother; she was the quintessential Jewish mother. She was so quintessential, she actually gave classes on Jewish motherdom. And she did that only because everyone treated her that way or saw her that way, so she decided to go with the flow rather than fight it. She was the spitting image of Molly Goldberg, a TV icon in the 50s on a show called, "The Goldbergs," and though you may not remember Molly, you might have heard her famous line, "I have to throw an eye in the soup." What astonished Rebecca was how many Jewish women signed up for her classes. They would give her the setup, and she would give them the payoff.

She was asked, "What is a Jewish mother's worst nightmare?" She answered, "Finding out her gay son is going out with a doctor."

Rebecca was also asked what a mother should say when her son who works in a strip joint brings home a photo on his cell phone of a topless dancer wearing only a red mini skirt and says, "This is the kind of girl I want to marry." Rebecca suggested, "That's the color I want for the chaise lounge."

Another mother asked her what information she should put on an identification card to be carried in her purse. Rebecca suggested, "In case of accident, I'm not surprised."

Another mother had a son who was trying to land a job as a chef at a Benihana restaurant. The applicants were tested on their expertise with knives: slicing and dicing, juggling them, using them to toss food onto plates, and manipulating them to beat a tattoo on the grill. She said she was going to accompany her son to the interview and asked what she could do to improve his chances. Rebecca said, "Take a cockroach with you and have your son flash his knives all around the insect. When the owner exclaims, 'You haven't touched him!' say quietly, 'He's circumcised.'"

Rebecca was asked what a mother should say if her daughter came home from school and asked her for $100 to go shopping at the mall with her friends. Rebecca said, "$75 dollars! You can't buy anything for $50 dollars!"

One of the mothers in the class told Rebecca she missed an "I-wish-I-had-said-that-at-the-time" moment when she sat down next to a man on a train and casually opined he was Jewish. He denied it. She said he dressed Jewish. He said no. She said he talked Jewish. He demurred. So she stared at him until he finally admitted he was Jewish. She asked Rebecca what she should have said at that exact moment, and Rebecca said, "That's odd. You don't look Jewish."

When other grandmothers shared pictures of their grandkids, one grandmother from Rebecca's class shared her son's business card. Learning that, Rebecca suggested she introduce her two grand-sons as, "The lawyer is five and the doctor is three."

Rocco

WHENEVER MY SISTER SAW ROCCO, she would think of Karen Carpenter singing, "On the day that you were born, the angels got together and decided to create a dream come true, so they sprinkled moon dust in your hair and golden starlight in your eyes of blue..." He was that gorgeous; he was that buff; he was the light heavyweight champion of the world at 27. His progress through the ranks was steady from joining a boxing club; to acquiring a trainer; to mastering the jab, uppercut and right hook; to fighting in the Olympics; and to battering his way up the professional ranks. Sadly, he was also punch drunk from starting his career too early.

He was invited to be the guest speaker at his former high school and said to his sparring partner, "I'm sposed to tell the kids everythin' I know about boxin'. What should I tell 'em?" His sparring partner said, "Tell 'em you got the mumps."

At the weigh-in before a title fight he exchanged fake punches with his challenger to excite the press crowding in around them and bragged, *sotto voce*, "See how popular I am." The challenger retorted, "You're about as popular as a snapping turtle in a bidet."

Speaking of bidets, as Rocco became more and more successful he was able to stay in better and better hotels while keeping the sophistication of his groupies about the same. He checked in with one of them on his arm and she squealed with delight as she inspected the luxury suite. She came into the living room and gushed, "My God, the toilet seat is heated and the lid goes up when you open the door! But what's the second toilet for?" Rocco said, " That ain't a toilet, it's a bidet, and it washes your bottom parts. You oughta try it." She did, was in the bathroom about an hour, returned to the living room flushed, and said in a husky voice, "I think I'm in love."

It was the very same groupie who, when asked by a hostile reporter what she saw in Rocco, said in all seriousness, "He can lick his eyebrows."

On the day of his wedding, Rocco's bride, another groupie, asked his Mom if she could speak to her confidentially and they stepped into an alcove so they could talk freely. The bride said, "What can I do to make your son happy?" His Mom replied, "Love him. Meet his needs. Excite him. Succor him. Your marriage will be beautiful." The bride said, "Look Mom, I know how to suck cock. I need you to teach me how to cook veal parmigiana."

Rocco tried to make the boxing team at a junior college before he dropped out of school forever. When he went into the gym the coach asked him how fit he was, how fast he could back-pedal, how quick his hands were, how much weight he could press, how many different punches he threw, how much stamina he had, and how much weight he carried. The coach was a great believer in joint training, not solo training, so when a medicine ball in the corner caught his eye, he said, "Can you pass a ball?" Rocco thought about it and said, "If I can gulp it, I can probably pass it."

Jarvis

JARVIS' GRANDFATHER WAS A WAITER, his father was a waiter, and he was a waiter. From the time he was nine, he loved to drape a folded napkin over his forearm and pretend he was serving food. His father and grandfather gave him all sorts of advice on how to speak knowledgeably, ask politely, suggest subtly, and carry efficiently. It did not hurt that he resembled, and moved with the same dignity as, everyone's preconceived notion of Jeeves the butler. As with any career, his moved up step-by-step from diner to five-star, and at 53 he was at the top of his game at one of San Francisco's finest eateries. It is true he exuded charm but, deep down, he was a wiseass.

I met him late one night after the last seating in his restaurant. He liked to enjoy a cocktail in the lounge before heading home and it was there we started talking. I was fascinated at how easily he made everyone he served feel like the most important person in the room. He told me about his family history and how devastated his mother was when his father died and how she asked a fortuneteller to try to reach him so she could speak to him. During the séance the air suddenly turned cold and his mother cried out, "Talk to me! Talk to me, Tom!" A distant voice replied, "Sorry, it's not my table."

Jarvis often waited on a society doyenne and after an expensive dinner and a skimpy tip helped her on with her coat and said, "I wish I had ten regulars just like you." She blushed and said, "Even though I tip poorly?" He replied, "Yes, I wish I had ten regulars just like you but, unfortunately, I have 300."

On another occasion, he was serving a gigantic fat man who was consuming copious amounts of food. The man swallowed faster than he could chew and asked Jarvis what he would recommend to wash the food down. Jarvis replied, "San Francisco Bay."

A particular raconteur whom Jarvis served frequently asked him to write some sincere but simple toasts for a large dinner party he was having at Jarvis' restaurant. Alas, Jarvis' wiseass streak intervened. For the boss, he wrote; "Here's hoping he never hears what we say about him." For the honoree, he wrote, "Who is more of an inspiration than Joe? If he can make it, anyone can." For the spouse he wrote, "She ages like wine. The older she gets the better she likes it." For the brother, he wrote, "He's finally decided to take a wife, but hasn't determined whose." And for the wives in the room, he wrote, "You will always be first in our thoughts and first in our billfolds."

Every now and then, Jarvis was asked to tend the bar in the lounge when they were short-staffed. He would listen sympathetically to customers' stories and this one from a depressed drunk was his favorite: The drunk and his wife were drinking champagne at a bar when they noticed that the man on the other side of the wife was doing the same. She said to him, "We're celebrating my pregnancy. How about you?" He said, "Sort of the same. I raise chickens and they were infertile until now." She asked, "What did you do?" He said, "I changed cocks." Without thinking, she gushed, "Me, too!"

Enid

ENID STARTED OUT AS A regular secretary with moderate skills but big ambitions. She knew she would not make much money staying where she was so, to her credit, she obtained a medical secretary degree, an office administrator degree, a business assistant degree, and a paralegal degree. It was not until she realized she was very comfortable with her secretarial skills, and received an offer to be the executive secretary to the CEO of a Fortune 500 company, that she realized she had finally found the job she wanted. By then she was 40, carried herself proudly, dressed with a finished look, and radiated confidence. But through it all, she was ever amazed at the human comedy.

She told me that in her younger days she was not above the office affair to advance her career and accepted an invitation to go to a vice president's house while his wife was away on vacation with her girlfriends. Passion was building when they realized neither of them brought condoms. The vice president had the bright idea of using his wife's diaphragm, thought he knew where it was, but could not find it after a thorough search of the house. When he returned to the bedroom he was furious and said, "What a shit! She has it with her. Now I know she doesn't trust me!"

There was also a fairly obnoxious guy at the office who kept asking Enid if she knew how to navigate dating websites to find the best babes. His question sort of implied she was lonely and desperate and probably spent a lot of time on such websites. She said if he would give her the particulars of what he was looking for, she would get him a photo of the perfect mate. He said, "I'm looking for a girl who dresses formally, is drop-dead cute, loves the ocean, and is comfortable in crowds." Ten minutes later Enid gave him a picture of a penguin.

Another time a sycophantic executive of the company rushed into her office and asked her help in dealing with a political problem. He said, "As you know, we're building a new factory downtown and there's going to be a huge ribbon-cutting ceremony with both the cardinal and the CEO attending. After the festivities they are coming back here to meet with me but my secretary screwed up and scheduled them both at the same time. She's not here now and I need you to greet them. Which one should I see first?" Enid thought about it and said, "The cardinal, I think. You only have to kiss his ring."

The best pickup line Enid heard from one of the executives waiting to see the CEO was, "Would you like scotch and sofa, or would you prefer gin and platonic?"

Enid became fast friends with Allison, the stewardess on the CEO's executive jet. Over dinner one night, Allison said, "I have a puzzle for you. We had a man on the plane who absolutely would not stop complaining. He complained the food was cold, the beverages were warm, the sound system had static, and the bathroom was always occupied. Guess what I told him?" Enid reflected a moment and opined, "Fly the goddamned plane and stop bitching!"

Spike

AT NO TIME DID SPIKE ever want to go straight. He jacked his first truck at 15; picked the pocket of his first mark at 18; got busted for selling drugs at 21; and served eight years in Attica for grand theft, auto. You might say he was perfecting his art; searching for his métier. It was as though he sat down at 31 and asked: "What crime involves no violence, no guns, no special equipment, no armed guards and no contact with victims?" Art forgery sounded good but he lacked the skill. Computer theft fit the bill but he lacked the training. So, he settled for being a burglar by the process of elimination and never looked back. His favorite pastime was tweaking the cops when the opportunity arose.

Spike was arrested on suspicion of robbing a jewelry store. It turns out he had an alibi, but he also was in the area of the crime. The cops asked him if he witnessed the robbery and he said he had. They asked him to describe it and he said the thief appeared to be a trained gorilla that drove up to the store, crashed in, scooped a lot of jewelry into its hands, jumped out, and drove away. The cop asked,

"Could you tell if it was a lowland gorilla or a mountain gorilla?" Spike said, "How should I know? It was wearing a Nixon mask."

Spike told me he had a recent scare when he burgled a house in an upscale neighborhood. As he was tiptoeing through the darkness, a shrill voice said, "I see you and so does the Almighty." He stopped dead in his tracks but could see nothing. After a minute, he continued moving toward the safe and the same voice said, "I see you and so does the Almighty." Now, he was pissed and went to confront the speaker. It turned out to be a parrot. He muttered to himself, "Christ, it's just a bird!" The parrot said, "Maybe so, but the Almighty is a Doberman."

For a short while, Spike worked with two gay thieves. He knew it would not be long- lasting because every time they broke into a house, they rearranged the furniture.

Spike also had to work with two teenagers for one particular job because he needed small bodies to crawl through narrow spaces. Someone set off an alarm and the police arrested the two kids but not Spike because he fled the scene just in time. He told them before the job, "No matter what, use your one phone call to reach my lawyer who will bail you out." I asked Spike if the lawyer got them out promptly and he said, "No, they ordered Chinese food."

Speedy Gonzales was Spike's crime name so he could say, "This won't hurt, did it?"

Finally, Spike told me about the time he was in court for an arraignment and was preceded by an 86-year-old woman who was charged with murder for throwing her 91-year-old husband off a balcony. She testified she caught him in bed with another woman. I asked Spike why she killed him that way and he said. "Well, she thought that if he could fuck at 91, he could probably fly, too."

Part 8

Patrick

PATRICK WAS A TOT WHEN he decided he wanted to be a fireman. His family gave him toy fire trucks for Christmas. At ten, he knew marine biology was for him. His family gave him scuba gear. At 13, he wanted to be the lead singer in a rock band. His family did not give him a microphone. Now, at 16, he is still dealing with acne, fear of girls, starting at quarterback, raising his C+ average, learning to drive, and mastering Twitter. If you accused him of watching too much TV or spending too much time on the computer, you would be understating the problem. If he ever needed hand surgery, embedding a cell phone in his palm would make him deliriously happy. If you could break him of his mordant attitude toward life, you would be a better man than I am.

Patrick told me about something he did which caused great problems for his family. He had said to his Dad, "I want to marry Julie when I'm older." His father said, "Sorry, son. Don't tell your mom, but Julie is your half sister." Six months later, having recovered from a broken heart, he told his Dad, "I want to marry Erica." His father said, "I hate to admit it, but Erica is your half sister, too." His mom found him crying in the garage and asked what was wrong. He said, "Dad says I can't marry Julie or Erica because of some bad things he did." His mom said, "Don't worry about it. He's not your father."

With a twinkle in his eye, Patrick asked me, "Guess what I got my older sister for her birthday?" I said, "I have no idea." He said, "A singing mammogram."

Before he took up football, Patrick was on the baseball team and his parents came to watch every game. When he was at the plate, the umpire called a ball a strike. Patrick gave him some lip. When he ran to first and was called out though safe, he complained bitterly. When the inning was over, his father came to him and said sharply, "Have you ever heard of good sportsmanship? Have you ever heard of being courteous and respectful to your elders? Do you think it's right to yell and scream at an umpire and question his judgment?" Abashed, Patrick mumbled, "I guess not." His father said, "Good, now tell your mother!"

Before he joined the football team, Patrick attended many of the home games. The stadium was usually packed but Patrick told me how he beat the system by finding a good seat after the game started. He said that last Saturday he saw an empty seat on the 50-yard line, went to it, and asked the guy in the next seat if it was taken. The guy said the seat was his wife's and they were both rabid football fans but sadly she passed away. Patrick commiserated, "I'm sorry, sir, but didn't any friends or family want to use the seat?" He said, "They're at the funeral."

Patrick's girlfriend invited him to dinner at her house with "first-time" sex afterward. He went to a pharmacist who helped him with everything from advice to equipment. At dinner, Patrick refused to look up and kept praying. His girlfriend whispered, "I didn't know you were so religious." He hissed, "I didn't know your father was a pharmacist!"

Maria

MARIA LEARNED A VALUABLE LESSON from her mother who had numerous ways of saying the same thing: Make hay while the sun shines; don't fiddle while Rome burns; don't sweat the small stuff; keep your eye on the prize; and don't let the grass grow under your feet. Her mother was referring to travel. She was bitter that she had seen so little of the world and urged Maria not to make the same mistake. So Maria toured the world and grew more skillful and more efficient at it until she realized she could make a living doing what she loved. Everyone wanted her as his or her tour guide because she was knowledgeable, smart, beautiful, and had a great sense of humor.

When she was my guide in Paris, she told me about an earlier trip to the city where an elderly woman died in her sleep. Her husband decided to bury her in Paris because it was her favorite city. He asked Maria where he could buy a black hat for the funeral and she told him how to find it and how to ask for it in French. His efforts went awry and he told Maria what had happened to him. She responded, "Oh my. No wonder you had difficulties. The taxi driver thought you wanted to buy a black condom. He took you to a seedy store. The clerk offered green, blue and black condoms. You picked black. The clerk asked why? You said your wife had died. He cried, 'My God, what a commitment!'"

Maria rented a double-decker bus in London to take a bunch of Mississippi Klansmen to see the city. She transited from the top deck to the bottom deck to ensure everyone was having fun. The folks on the bottom deck were partying like crazy but the ones on the top deck sat quietly, looked fearful, and held tightly to the bars on the seats in front of them. One Klansman from the bottom deck came upstairs and asked Maria, " Why aren't they partying?" She shouted over the traffic, "They don't have a driver!"

Maria also developed a nice arsenal of rejoinders to the pick up lines inevitably proffered by oversexed men on her tours. If the guy was obnoxious and asked her for a date, she said, "Sorry, I don't date outside my species." If he was cocky and asked what she did for a living, she said, "I'm a female impersonator." If he was pre-sumptuous and asked how she liked her eggs in the morning, she said, "Unfertilized." If he was overconfident and asked her to come back to his place, she asked, "Will two people fit under your rock?" If he was insufferable and said he would die happy if he could see her naked, she said, "If I could see you naked, I'd die laughing." If he was unendurable and said he wanted to get into her pants, she said, "Sorry, but there's already one asshole in there." And if he was self-righteous and said she knocked him dead with her looks, she said, "You knock me dead with your breath."

Maria told me about her worst tour ever. Her bus broke down in the Sahara and she and her passengers, all men, started hiking. Three days later, dying of thirst, they found a shack but the guy only had ties for sale. So, they trudged five miles more to another shack that supposedly had water, but when they arrived, half dead, the owner would not let them in. I asked why and Maria replied, "He said they couldn't come in without ties."

Arthur

IT IS KIND OF RIDICULOUS to call Arthur a delivery boy when he is almost 30, but the moniker seems to get him bigger tips than would otherwise occur if he shouted out "Delivery Man" or "Delivery Person." As manufacturers ship more and more of their goods directly to customers, and the need for delivery boys shrinks accordingly, the field becomes ever more competitive. But Arthur is able to compete on price because he is willing to work for slave wages; and he is willing to work for slave wages because he is a bit slow on the uptake. So long as he has a roof over his head, some food, and enough money to make payments on his scooter, he is happy.

I first made his acquaintance sitting next to him at a bar where he was trying to pick up a lady sitting to his other side. Apparently, he was fairly shy in settings like this so the lady had to do most of the work encouraging him and giving him confidence he would not be rejected. He bought her one drink after another, kept the conversation lighthearted, and apparently received some very good vibes so, mustering his courage, he asked her if she would like to go back to his place. She turned to him with a beautiful smile and said, "I'd love to, but I have my cycle." He brightened considerably and said, "That's okay. I have my Honda. You follow me!"

That was not his first hustling experience in that bar. He spotted a classy lady across the room one night and felt he did not stand a chance without some chemical assistance. He had just heard about Spanish fly and asked the bartender if he had any. The bartender said, "No, I only carry Jewish fly." Figuring one was as good as the other, he said to the bartender, "Look, when she orders her next drink, pour some fly in it and tell her it's on me, okay?" The bartender complied, she drank it, and within minutes she was as itchy as a cat on a hot tin roof. Arthur's hopes soared when she came over and whispered erotically in his ear, "Let's go shopping."

Arthur would often converse with the dispatcher at his delivery company. He admired the man because of his years of experience and helpful advice. On one occasion, the dispatcher was telling Arthur about his worst scooter accident. He said, "I was parked between two vans with my front tire touching the curb. The van in front pulled away and a lady driving a Lincoln tried to back into the space, smashed into my scooter, and crushed it. I couldn't stop screaming and called her every name in the book." Utterly amazed, Arthur asked, "There's a book?"

On another occasion, one of Arthur's gay co-workers came to work driving a beautiful, new scooter. Since the co-worker made as little money as he did, Arthur could not help wonder how he was able to acquire such a gem. His co-worker said, "I went to my favorite bar last night and caught the eye of a really cute guy. We drank together and went out into the parking lot to get our scooters. His was magnificent. Before I could praise it, he ripped off all of his clothes and said, 'Everything I have is yours.'" Arthur reflected and said, "I think you made the right choice. I doubt his clothes would have fit."

Pete

IF YOU EARNED A B.A. in philosophy, a masters in the history of science, and a doctorate in physics, one would assume your career path would follow one or more of those disciplines. If, at the same time, you were a philosopher king, a bemused student of the human condition, and a devotee of the church of cheekiness, you would do what Pete did: you would become a garbage collector. Thus, the world was yours to survey from a lofty perch; time was sufficiently unregulated to indulge your writing; and the calling was quirky enough to fascinate the opposite sex. It did not hurt that he was also 25, a cross between Brad Pitt and George Clooney, and double whip-smart.

I first met Pete when his truck was collecting garbage in our neighborhood and something occurred that convinced me he was not your standard sanitation employee. He picked up the trash from our next-door neighbor's house and was moving down the street when she rushed out of the house wearing only her ancient bathrobe over a ratty nightgown with curlers in her hair and white makeup on her face. She carried a bag of garbage and yelled to Pete, "You forgot about me!" Without missing a beat, he shouted, "Hop on, lady!"

We often had philosophical arguments about the rankings of the professions. We discussed which were the most useful to society, which the most useless, and which the most replaceable. He gave me this hypothetical: "Suppose I died and wound up at the pearly gates with a historian and a lawyer and St. Peter decided to test us to see who was worthy of admittance. Suppose he asked the historian what was the first ocean liner sunk in World War I and he correctly named the Lusitania and was admitted to heaven. Suppose he then asked me, a garbage collector, how many people died on the Lusitania and I correctly said 1,118 and was admitted to heaven. What do you suppose he would have then asked the lawyer?" I shrugged and Pete said, "Name them!"

Pete's life was rarely perfume and roses. In fact, it could be quite odiferous. After being told how he made his living, a turned-on beauty yearned to have sex with him and asked him when he was free. Pete said, "I work Tuesday through Saturday. How about Sunday?" She countered, "How about Monday?"

On one of his rounds, Pete noticed some plywood with a hole in the center filling the front window of the house across the street from ours. He asked me what happened. I said, "A wild couple lives there and they had a party last night where the men had to put their genitals through the hole and the women had to guess who it was." Pete said, "I'm sorry I wasn't there." I said, "Technically, you were. Your name came up five times."

Finally, there are the deep philosophical questions Pete is currently pondering: "If a tree falls in the forest, is it still the man's fault?" "Do people with psychic powers get nostalgic about next week?" "What if there were no hypothetical questions?" "Can atheists get insurance for acts of God?" And "Are complete pessimists positively negative?"

Cyrus

AT SIX, CYRUS WANTED TO be an emissary; at 10, a legate; at 13, a consul; at 16, an envoy; at 20, a charge d'affaires; and at 24, a full-blown ambassador. He took the written exam for the Foreign Service in Washington and passed with flying colors. But the oral exam in New York at the Offices of the United States Ambassador to the United Nations did not go as well, and though he was admitted to the Service, he was still just a regular diplomat 25 years later. Certainly, he handled his duties with competence and professionalism, but because he was a tad bitter and could be rather acerbic, his battle to suppress his inner demons was continuous.

It was at a NATO conference in Brussels where Cyrus's diplomatic one-upmanship was first put to the test. He was having lunch with a French diplomat and an Italian diplomat and the talk turned, as guy-talk invariably does, to sexual prowess. The French diplomat boasted that he made love three times to a headquarters secretary the night before and she raved about his stamina in the morning. The Italian diplomat noted he made love five times to the English ambassador's assistant the night before and she lauded his endurance in the morning. Cyrus said nothing until asked, "Did you make love to anyone last night and, if, so, how many times?" He said, "Yes, to a general's wife, and only once." "Only once?" the diplomats sputtered, "What did she say in the morning?" Cyrus arched an eyebrow and said, "Please don't stop."

Cyrus is well known for describing a rival diplomat as, "The human equivalent of beige."

By happenstance, Cyrus looked a lot like Frank Sinatra and was often mistaken for him at public functions. He would have to insist "I am not Frank" over and over again to calm unruly crowds. Several years ago, when Frank was still alive, I was with Cyrus at the opening of new consular offices in Bodrum, Turkey, where he was mistaken for Frank once again; only this time it was not by a boisterous crowd but by two beautiful young women who pleaded with him to join them in a *ménage a' trois*. He stopped dead in his tracks, turned to them, and crooned, "Scooby dooby doo…"

I once asked Cyrus, "You travel the globe so often, have you ever lost your luggage?" He said, "Just once. I landed at Heathrow in London but my bags were sent to Israel." I asked, "Was everything there when you got them back?" He said, "Yes, but the pants were altered."

During a stint at the United Nations, Cyrus was asked to design a series of questions for other diplomats to answer that would elicit responses demonstrating cultural differences. The question he devised that proved the most efficacious was: "What is your opinion of the world's scarcity of beef?" The Dubai diplomat asked, "Please, but what is scarcity?" The Samoan diplomat asked, "Please, but what is beef?" The Russian diplomat asked, "Please, but what is an opinion?" And the French diplomat asked, "Please, but what is 'please?'"

Farouk

Farouk was orphaned at five in the coup that overthrew the monarchy in Egypt and brought Gamal Abdel Nasser to power in 1952. He lived a street urchin's life thereafter, moving from one Mideast country to another until he was so thoroughly disillusioned with all aspects of Arab politics, wars and religions, that he craved a quieter, non-involved, more reflective way of life; so he decided to become a camel driver at 18 and roam the endless, wind-swept deserts of northern Africa. I first met him when I was on a Jeep Safari in the Sahara. By then he was an old man eager to tell his tales. I did find it difficult, however, to differentiate fact from fancy, sincerity from sarcasm.

He told me that he attended the school of hard knocks to learn his trade. He was invited to join a seven-day caravan provided he brought his own camel. He had saved a little money and went to buy his first one. He told the merchant he needed a camel that could survive for seven days without water and was assured it would be so. After four days, the camel died and Farouk, playing hell getting back through the desert, berated the merchant for cheating him. The merchant asked, "Did you 'brack' the camel?" Farouk said, "No," The merchant said, "Well, that explains it. To turn a 4-day camel into a 7-day camel you have to walk behind him with a couple of bricks while he's drinking water and smash his balls with the bricks. The sucking sound will be your extra 3-day supply."

For five years Farouk tended camels at a fort run by the French Foreign Legion. The fighting and transport camels were kept in tip-top shape but a scruffy one was used for local trips. A new Colonel demanded Farouk get rid of it but reversed himself when Farouk said, "Well sir, when the men get horny..." The Colonel interrupted him and said, "Fine, fine, of course, I understand." Late one night six months later, a very drunk and very randy Colonel was servicing the scruffy camel when Farouk walked in and the Colonel slurred, "Is this how the men do it?" Farouk said, "No, sir, they usually ride it to the whorehouse in town."

Although Farouk was retired, he still took his one camel to the town well to wash it every morning. I watched him one day and through-out the morning people came by and asked him the time of day. He would nod, bend over, wash the camel's balls for a while, and then announce the time. I could not resist and had to ask Farouk how he did it. He told me to bend down and watch. I did, he washed the camel's balls, and then he pushed the scrotal sac to one side and said, "See the clock on the tower over there...?"

On overnight trips, Farouk provided his guests with all the camp-ing amenities they would need at the oasis. Most were grateful; a few were oblivious. On one trip, he shared sleeping quarters with an astronomer and woke him up in the middle of the night to ask him what he saw. Assuming Farouk was testing his expertise, the astronomer waxed eloquent about galaxies and stars, planets and moons, and the size and age of the universe. Farouk was silent and the astronomer asked him what he saw when he looked up? Farouk said quietly, "Some asshole stole our tent!"

Vivian

VIVIAN SIMPLY COULD NOT KEEP her stories straight because she was a lush. Ten years earlier, at 40, she had a beautiful family, a luxurious house, and a challenging but satisfying career. Then everything went to hell and she still cannot explain why. Drop by drop her life came apart. The kids left for college and became cynical know-it-alls. Her husband died and his partner cheated her out of her share of the business. She survived a bout with cancer but was left weak and listless. And her house was taken in foreclosure. At first she fought with grit and determination, then pills, then booze. She was grateful for two things: She did not take the road to hell using drugs; and she never lost her sense of humor.

To maintain supply, Vivian worked as a bartender in a lounge called "The Golden Goblet." It was famous for covering all its furniture, fixtures and equipment with gold leaf. One evening when we were chitchatting, she received a call and put it on speaker so she could hear over the band. A woman asked, "Is this where everything is covered in gold?" Vivian said, "Yes." The woman said, "Everything? The floor, the ceiling, the tables, the chairs?" Vivian said, "That's right." The woman said, "My husband claims even the urinals are covered in gold." At that, Vivian put her hand over the mouthpiece and shouted to the band, "Tommy, it's for you. I think it's the wife of the guy who pissed in your sax last night!"

Vivian insisted alcohol was good for one's health. Her uncle drank ten glasses of vodka every day and lived to be 94. She noted, however, that when he passed away, she went to his cremation and, try as they might, they could not put out the fire.

Investment bankers would describe Vivian's stumbling attempts to get home every night as a true "random walk." I came upon her late one night under a street lamp searching for something on her hands and knees. She was very distressed. I dropped down and asked if I could help. She said, "Oh God, I lost my diamond ring up the block." I said, "If you lost your ring up the block, why are you searching here?" She looked at me as though I were dense, and said, "Obviously, the light's better here, twit!"

Vivian swears this story is true: She was closing the bar one night and there was a scratching at the door and when she opened it she encountered a turtle begging for a drink. His pleading was so cloying it got on her nerves and she slammed the door in his face shouting, "We don't serve turtles!" Six months later there was a scratching at the door and when Vivian opened it, it was the same turtle. It slowly lifted its head, laboriously turned its neck to look up, and said, "That wasn't very nice."

I came out of a store one day and discovered I was walking ten feet behind Vivian who was swaying down the street. Two priests approached her and split up to go around her. When I caught up with her, she had a puzzled look on her face, and said, "I wonder how he did that?"

Rex

REX WAS NOT A PARANOID schizophrenic. He was just paranoid. Though both disorders involve withdrawal from others, Rex did not have hallucinations. He was a just a patient who had delusions that some person or some individuals were plotting either against him or against members of his family. He was guarded and suspicious and led a constricted emotional life, which was not easy for a greeter at Wal-Mart. He took that counterintuitive job to fight for his sanity: to not go quietly into the good night, but to rage, rage against the dying of the light. So, at 25, he was a chubby, excessively gregarious greeter, pretending mirth but cringing on the inside.

Rex told me he first suspected his affliction when he was walking home from a youth clinic and stopped to watch some workers at a construction site. He closed his eyes to listen to the din and discovered the riveter was calling him a psycho in Morse code.

He mused, "It's odd how paranoia can link up with reality now and then." He asserted, "Just because you're paranoid doesn't mean an elephant isn't sitting on your face." He declared, "Of course I'm being persecuted whenever I'm contradicted." He conceded, "I may or may not be paranoid, but just to be on the safe side, I never go to sleep with an ostrich in the room." And he confided, "For sure my therapist believes I'm paranoid. He won't say it, but he thinks it."

Rex was institutionalized for a short while when his paranoia got out of hand. He shared a room with a slightly delusional patient who liked to play "light bulb." It was felt it would be therapeutic for Rex to assemble imaginary Lego structures to calm his paranoia. It was felt it would be therapeutic for his roommate to assume poses that satisfied his need to glow. A clinician walked into their room one day while Rex was building an imaginary bridge and his roommate was hanging from the doorway in anti-gravity inversion boots. The clinician asked Rex what his roommate was doing and Rex said, "He's believes he's a light bulb." The clinician said, "He should come down before he gets hurt." Rex barked, "Bullshit, I'm not going to work in the dark!"

Rex called his dog a "paranoid retriever." I asked why and he said, "Whenever we play fetch, he brings back everything."

Rex is also obsessed with insects, Whenever he travels, he asks that his hotel room be specially treated before he arrives. He gets down on hands and knees looking for cockroaches. He rubs baseboards with antiseptic wipes to kill ants. He brings his own freshly laundered sheets to avoid bedbugs. When I asked why the obsession, he said, "I just don't want to be taken advantage of while I'm sleeping."

Before Rex joined Wal-Mart, he tried to take jobs that would give him a chance to help others similarly afflicted, but that did not work out so well. He was immediately fired after saying, "Welcome to the paranoia hot line. Please hold while we trace your call."

Dudley

So tell me, what is a nerd like Dudley doing in federal prison? With a name like that he certainly was not arrested for armed robbery, or assault with intent to kill, or aircraft hijacking. No, it was something far more mundane. It was simple accounting fraud. And it happened even though he was not trying to enrich himself. He was just a timid soul and when the Chief Financial Officer of the public company he worked for told him to cook the books, it never occurred to him to refuse or become a whistleblower. He just hoped for the best right up to the time the FBI raided his office and put him in handcuffs. So there he was, a felon in prison, with the next 20 years of his 31-year-old life permanently on ice, but, fortunately, an attitude fatalistic enough to survive.

After Dudley served about five years, he was assigned a newly convicted cellmate who wanted to know how the prisoners spent their week. Dudley said, "On weekends we attend religious services. On Monday we play Scrabble. On Tuesday we exercise in the yard. On Wednesday we do laundry. On Thursday..." His cellmate interrupted him, "How fucking boring!" Dudley said, "Maybe, but do you like sex with women" "His cellmate said, "Damn right!" Dudley said, "Well, I don't think you're going to like Fridays."

Dudley was a ringleader in a prison riot and got five years in solitary confinement along with two other agitators. The warden said they could take one item with them into their cells. The first agitator asked for medical books and when he emerged he was ready to graduate medical school. The second agitator was smart enough to ask for a hooker and when he emerged he had three kids. Dudley asked for 300 boxes of cigars and when he emerged he said, "Anyone got a light?"

For a short while Dudley shared a cell with a former carpenter who was offered a reduced sentence if he rebuilt and refit the counters in the prison kitchen. He refused and this surprised everyone because it was such a favorable trade-off. Another prisoner asked Dudley why he did it and Dudley said, "Well, it was counter fitting that got him in trouble in the first place."

I was an observer at Dudley's trial where he was charged with both market manipulation and accounting fraud. I visited him in prison and he told me he spotted a ditzy blonde on the jury whom he bribed to try to get one of the two charges dropped for a lighter sentence. I asked him if it worked and he said, "Yes. I was only convicted of accounting fraud. After the trial I asked her how she managed it. She told me, 'It was very, very hard. They wanted to acquit you.'"

While serving his time, Dudley met a coroner briefly jailed for contempt of court; he pissed off a judge. Dudley asked him what happened. He said, "The Judge asked me if I examined the deceased. I said 'No.' He asked, 'Well, did you check his pulse?' I said, 'No.' Now annoyed, he asked, 'Did you try to revive him at all?' I said 'No.' He yelled, 'Then how did you know he was dead?' I answered, 'His brain was in a jar.'"

Stanford

WHEN STANFORD REALIZED HE NEVER had any intention of keeping his promises, he knew he wanted to be a politician. He practiced his profession with great skill and was amazed election after election that he was never punished for breaking his promises. No matter how much bullshit he doled out, the morons believed him. He could now understand how demagogues got their start, and vowed that should he ever become president, he would pass a constitutional amendment giving him the office for life. But the presidency was far in the future, and for now he was just a slick, glad-handing, 45-year-old "pol" with an eye on the prize and contempt in his heart.

I interviewed him after a press conference and he told me about a very satisfying event that occurred earlier in the day. He was strolling through the park with a doctor and an architect. They were walking their dogs and bragging about how smart they were. The doctor called his dog Artery over, dropped a bag of bones from the butcher on the ground, and watched the dog assemble them into the shape of a man. The architect called his dog Rivet over and watched him reassemble the bones into the shape of a man standing. I asked Stanford how his dog could top that? He said, "I called Martini over, he ate the bones, fucked the other two dogs, and took the afternoon off."

Stanford realized that immigration was a hot button issue and looked for ways to exploit it. When he was with Christians he blamed the Muslims, when he was with whites he blamed the blacks, when he was with blacks he blamed the Latinos, and when he was with Latinos he blamed the Asians. He slipped up one day and revealed his true feelings. He told a crowd, "All of the troubles we face today can be attributed to the uninformed immigration strategies of the American Indian."

He always tried to conform his speeches to what he believed the crowds wanted to hear. No matter what position he had on any issue, it was completely reversible by the polls. He judged the effectiveness of his speeches by the questions he was asked. At one rally, after boasting about his many virtues, he was taken aback when a listener asked, "Who's running against you?"

In mid-career he was so disgusted with his party he urged its caucus to change its symbol from an elephant to a prophylactic because it relies on inflation, stifles passion, interferes with production, shields pricks, and screws others in complete safety.

Sometimes I wondered if there was any limit to how low he could go. To win the senior vote, he promised cash advances on Social Security.

Stanford talked about death a lot, mainly in terms of taking revenge on his enemies, not about leaving a positive legacy. He said to me, "Just before I die I'm going to switch from being a Republican to being a Democrat." I asked, "Why?" and he answered, "Because it's better one of them die than one of us."

Part 9

Ivy

Ivy WAS A SPY AND to use a trite descriptive phrase she was "built like a brick shithouse." She flunked out of the FBI Academy for being a little too dim and by rights her career in intelligence should have been over, but the CIA was ramping up its *Honey Trap* program at the time and it was felt the benefits of her seductiveness would outweigh the burdens of her cluelessness. She was a ravishing, head-turning, 26-year-old fox, and the speed with which she entrapped informants and spies was astonishing. Fortunately for her, she viewed sex as nothing more than mechanics, so she had no particular qualms or regrets about bedding down with some fairly unattractive or unsavory characters. And to her credit, she was very good at keeping her occupation a secret.

On one of her first assignments, Ivy entrapped an Italian naval attaché who was using his position to supply NATO military secrets to the Russians. The operation was carried out so deftly, he had no idea it was Ivy who turned him in and he still considered her a friend. The CIA wanted to use him as a double agent and they grilled him continuously for a month but he would not talk. They returned him to Ivy to find out why. He told Ivy what happened and how steadfast he was. She asked how he managed not to talk and he said, "I wanted to, but they cuffed me and I couldn't move my hands."

On another occasion, Ivy was asked to extract three CIA spies out of Bulgaria: One was an Italian Catholic, one was an Irish American, and one was an Israeli Jew. It was felt she would not be conspicuous meeting them in a bar near the border and guiding them on a long hike to safety. She was in far better shape than they were and after ten miles the Italian said, "I'm exhausted and parched. I must have wine." The American said, "I'm exhausted and parched. I must have beer." The Israeli said, "I'm exhausted and parched. I must have diabetes."

Ivy was asked to recruit a particular spy in a small village in Asia. Because he was so devoted to his dog, it was suggested she approach him through that common interest. She met him "by coincidence" in a bar where he was sitting with a dog at his feet. She gushed, "You have a beautiful dog. Does he bite?" He said "No", so she reached down to pet it and the dog savagely bit her wrist. She shrieked, "You said your dog didn't bite!" He replied coolly, "It's not my dog."

Ivy told me she had a dream where an angel granted her one wish, so she asked to live forever. The angel said that was too long, so Ivy asked, "How about until Congress gets its head out of its ass?" The angel smiled, "Clever girl."

After a few years of service Ivy was asked to teach a class to new *Honey Trap* recruits about a recently approved intelligence-gathering program. She told them that under the program, the target was never to know how his computer was hacked, how his bank account was manipulated, how his civil liberties were violated, or how his sexual preferences were exploited. She said, "We call the program 'Immaculate Collection.'"

Dakshi

A SWAMI, FROM THE SANSKRIT, is an ascetic or yogi who has been initiated into a religious monastic order founded by a religious teacher. The usage of the word is not just for a yogi but also for a religious guru, with or without disciples. It can mean master, lord or prince, and is used by Hindus as a term of respectful address, or in some cases, it is the idol or temple of a god. Dakshi is a swami. He grew up in abject poverty in Calcutta and joined his first order at 16. As the years passed and he became ever wiser and ever more learned, he started to find a lot of what he thought and taught was funny. Not disrespectful: just funny. Not iconoclastic: just funny.

When I was on a religious pilgrimage to India, he told me of an event that gave him his first profound understanding of his faith. He was studying in a monastery high in the Himalayas when he walked onto a large balcony and joined several gurus who were taking in an incredible scene. The sun was setting behind the snow-capped mountains, giving the sky a stunning golden hue, while shafts of sunlight pierced both the mountain passes and the clouds and lit up the valleys below. As they watched, the gurus applauded quietly and cried softly, "Author! Author!"

I told Dakshi that during my pilgrimage I learned God existed before the creation and would exist after the end of time. He observed, "Imagine trying to stay awake during his home movies!"

He asked me, "How many Taoists does it take to screw in a light bulb?" I said, "How many?" He said, "Three. One to screw in the light bulb, one not to screw in the light bulb, and one to have a mystical experience."

Dakshi told me he was in Africa preaching unto men their divinity and how to make it manifest in every movement of life, while at the very same time he was harboring doubts about his faith. He was crossing the Congo River when he was seized by a sea serpent that held him in its mouth and tried to drag him under. He cried out, "God, please save me!" God replied, "I thought you believed I didn't exist?" He yelled, "Cut me some slack, will you? Ten minutes ago I didn't believe in sea serpents, either."

Dakshi attended an interfaith conference and had dinner with a priest, a mullah and a rabbi who talked about how their faith had been restored by God. The priest said, "I was on a boat that was sinking in a terrible storm and I asked Christ to save us. Suddenly, for a mile around us the sea was calm and we made it to safety. I've always believed since then." The mullah said, "I was caught in a massive fire near an oil refinery and I asked Allah to save us. Suddenly, for a mile around us the fire went out and we were able to crawl to safety. I never doubted again." The rabbi said, "I was leaving temple when I discovered a million dollars in a sack on the steps of the temple but couldn't take it because it was the Sabbath. I asked Jehovah for help. Nothing happened. Then, suddenly, for a mile around us, it was Thursday."

Sloopy

Sloopy attended Ringling. Bros. and Barnum & Bailey Clown College, which trained around 1,400 clowns in the "Ringling style" from 1968 to 1997. His classes included make-up, costume design, acrobatics, juggling, stilt walking and pantomime. He was a star student and was asked to join the circus after graduation, and his personal style emphasized broad and slapstick humor. It was not surprising he became a clown because he started entertaining others at parties, receptions and festivals at six years of age. He loved being the center of attention; he loved putting smiles on people's faces; and he loved jerking people around.

Sloopy and his fellow students were asked what they would do if they drove by a car stopped for running a red light, which was being driven by a clown skilled at juggling, who was asked by the cop to demonstrate what his swords were for, and who got out of the car to perform his juggling act that was both amazing and dangerous. The instructor asked the class, ""How would you react to this scene?" Sloopy piped up and said, "I would say, 'Jesus Christ, no more booze for me! I'll never pass that test!'"

When I met Sloopy in mid-career, he was considering becoming a wild-animal trainer to enhance his portfolio. He auditioned for the job along with a beautiful young woman. She stepped into the cage with a chair and a whip and when the tiger charged she opened her coat to show him she was completely naked. The tiger stopped, crawled to her, and licked her from head to toe. The ringmaster asked Sloopy, "Can you do that?" He answered, "Goddamn right! Ditch the tiger."

During one circus performance, Sloopy was horribly constipated and, after the show, rushed to the drug store in his clown costume to buy a laxative. To conform his clothes to his dilemma, he whispered to the druggist, "I'm here for comic relief."

A year later we were drinking in a sports bar when a commercial for a new drug came on that was ludicrous because the warnings about its side effects took longer than the claims for its benefits. I pointed this out to Sloopy and he said, "Yeah, but I take the warnings seriously. I don't want to get a yeast infection."

Sloopy shared the clown tent with Oliver, a tone-deaf jester, who wanted to learn the violin so he could be promoted to the circus orchestra. When he practiced, the violin's screeching sounded like fingernails across a blackboard and it set Oliver's dog Ruff to howling. Finally, a frustrated Sloopy cried out, "God damn it, Oliver, can't you play something Ruff doesn't know?"

Sloopy's fellow clown Ernie was, sadly, less than swift. They were watching a car chase in a movie on TV and Sloopy bet Ernie $100 the lead car would hit a wall. It did. Feeling guilty, Sloopy confessed, "You know, I've seen that movie before." Ernie said, "I did, too. I just didn't think the schmuck would do it twice."

Danny

DANNY RESEARCHES EVERY SYMPTOM HE has on the internet. He is convinced minor ailments are actually major diseases. He feels fine but is constantly worried about getting sick. He keeps worrying even after a doctor tells him he is healthy. He visits multiple doctors for second opinions. And he is convinced any illness he has will progress. He has a somatic symptom disorder which used to be called "hypochondria." It is sad that a perfectly fit 50-year-old has had to battle with various imaginary health demons most of his life. But Danny is also sharp enough to know his affliction is absurd, and though he cannot help himself, he can laugh at himself.

Danny told me that the incident that set him on the road to hypochondria occurred when he was around 20. Unfortunately, he was consulting an insensitive quack who told him after an exam one day that he had both good news and bad news for him. The bad news was that he had only six months to live. Mortified, Danny asked, "What's the good news?" The doctor said, "Did you see that nurse outside who is an incredible piece of ass?" "I did." "Did you notice the big breasts and scrumptious bottom?" "Yes." "Did you notice the lush, raven hair and big blue eyes?" "Yes." "Well, I'm screwing her."

For a short while Danny was utterly despondent because he thought his wife was cheating on him. When he combined that with his hypochondria, suicide became an option. He knew he did not have the courage to do it himself, but thought he could provoke someone into doing it for him. When he found a matchbbook cover from a local bar in his wife's purse, he bought a gun, went into the bar, waved the gun in the air, and shouted, "I've got a Glock 23 pistol with ten rounds of 40 Smith & Wesson in the clip and one round in the chamber, and I want to know who's been sleeping with my wife." A voice from the back yelled, "You're gonna need more bullets!"

A number of the physicians Danny consulted tried to cure him with shock therapy. When he visited one physician imagining he had a bad cold, the physician prescribed aspirin knowing it would not work. Later, he prescribed shots knowing they would have no effect. Finally, he suggested Danny take a scalding shower and then stand nude in the snow. Danny exclaimed, "But I'll get the flu!" The doctor said, "*That* I can cure!"

Danny also confessed to me, "I know I'm a hypochondriac, but only because I've got a brain disorder." Months later, he went to a lecture at the Hypochondriac Society but was bitterly disappointed when the speaker called in sick. If I questioned his sincerity, he would insist, "Hypochondria is the only disease I haven't got!" And he confidently told one of his doctors, "I looked up my symptoms on the internet and believe I am dead."

Because Danny was so preoccupied with death, he gave a lot of thought to what his tombstone should say after he died. He considered sincere epitaphs, funny epitaphs, universal epitaphs, and philosophical epitaphs. But in the end he settled on one that reflected his travails in life. It said, "I told you I was sick. Assholes!"

Phyllis

PHYLLIS IS THE ORIGINAL HUMAN resources Princess of Darkness: the nation's leading consultant on reductions-in-force, plant closings, layoffs, downsizing, and terminations. All her clients are in the Fortune 500. She graduated with honors from Georgetown University and the University of Pennsylvania 40 years ago. She helped implement a major bureaucratic reorganization in Philadelphia, and served as vice president of a head hunting consulting firm in South Chicago. She also directed the corporate training and development function for two major banks. She is now a leading consultant and a certified bitch.

Phyllis recommended to a client that he schedule his weekly staff meetings for 4:45 on Friday afternoons. She said, "That's the only time the jerks won't argue with you."

She established her consulting firm with two other founders. They determined their percentage of ownership in proportion to their investments. Phyllis took 55%, the second founder took 42%, and the third founder took 3%. The third founder was made Director of Copulation and Inquiry. When he asked why, Phyllis said, "Don't give me any fucking advice until I ask for it." He still demanded a more prestigious title so she gave him "Vice President of Discontinued Operations, With Offices In The Field."

Phyllis told me her favorite opening line at surprise exit interviews was, "I have great news for you. You're about to have lots of time and anguish to write the novel you always daydreamed about." To comfort terminated employees, she said, "One day you'll look back on all this and say, 'I wish I had swiped more office supplies.'" And to a leading candidate for termination, she said, "We need you to test our severance package."

When Phyllis was starting out as a young human resources executive at a large corporation, she was called into the gay CEO's office and he asked her, "Do you know Bart Rodgers, the vice president of preliminary design?" "She said, "Yes, I've met him." He said, "Are you close to him?" She said, "Not really." He asked, "Did you ever sleep with him?" Startled, she said, "No, of course not." He said, "You're sure?" She said, "Absolutely!" He said, "Good. You fire him."

Phyllis admired Dr. Jack Kevorkian, the medical pathologist who willfully helped dozens of terminally ill people end their lives. She called him a "Transition Consultant."

When a distressed staffer rushed into Phyllis's office and declared, "Google has just laid off 1,000 employees!" Phyllis commented dryly, "I hope they backed them up before they deleted them."

Finally, Phyllis was not entirely without sympathy. To motivate employees who were not laid off, she said, "Be glad you didn't make enough money to be eligible for termination."

Barclay

IF YOU WANT TO BECOME an electrician, you need to enter a program that will give you proper course work in safety, code, equipment, and trade knowledge. Instruction will include fundamentals of electricity and power distribution; basic trade mathematics; national code requirements; commercial, industrial, and residential wiring requirements; and other control theory and fundamentals. Barclay never actually wanted to be an electrician. He wanted to be a concert pianist. But if it was not one thing, it was another, and he wound up a stocky, hirsute, myopic 33-year-old electrician with a chip on his shoulder and bitterness in his heart.

On one of his very first jobs for a very obnoxious lady, he approached her front door and knocked softly. She flung the door open and upbraided him saying, "What the hell are you doing here this morning? You were supposed to fix the doorbell two days ago." He smiled and said, "I tried. I rang the doorbell five times but no one answered, so I figured no one was home and left."

I interviewed Barclay for his second job as an electrician. After chatting a while about his training and his goals, I asked him if he had any other skills that might enhance his value to the company and enable him to work more quickly and efficiently. He said, "Yes. I wrote a concerto last year and learned to play the clavichord." I replied, "That's quite an accomplishment, but I was thinking more along the lines of abilities you might use on the job." He said, "Those *were* on the job."

Early in his career Barclay worked as a lineman for Pacific Gas & Electric in California, but the job did not last long. Because of the great need for linemen, the company's human resources department allowed people to go to work before their background checks were completed. They eventually got around to carefully reviewing Barclay's credentials and discovered he claimed to have worked on the wiring for NASA's shuttle, to have strung Christmas lights along the entire length of the Golden Gate Bridge, and to have installed all the night lighting at Aspen Ski Mountain. He was called into the vice president's office who growled, "It was all bullshit. You have nowhere near the qualifications needed for the job. Why did you do it?" Barclay calmly replied, "I believe you said you were looking for someone with an active imagination."

Late one night when Barclay was in his cups, he shared with me the wit and wisdom of the electrician: He said he once mistakenly blew the power to an ice-making factory forcing them to liquidate. He confessed that when his wife complained their relationship had lost its spark, he tasered her. He counseled that one should never trust an electrician without eyebrows. He noted the best definition of a shock absorber is a careless electrician. He said that when a superconductor walks into a restaurant where it is not welcome, it leaves without resistance. And he claimed the very best motto he ever heard for his profession was, "Good judgment comes from experience. Experience comes from bad judgment."

Chas

IT DID NOT MATTER TO Chas if he was selling encyclopedias, Tupperware, vacuums, storm drains, cable services, alarm systems or water filtration equipment: He just loved going door-to-door and meeting/conning new people. He mastered the basics of his trade early: Acquire a free sample of the product; create a flyer stating the price of the product or service; obtain training from the manufacturer or service supplier; practice in the mirror over and over; know your customer; knock, knock, knock on doors; and be prepared for rejection. It did not hurt that he resembled a Choir Boy exuding sincerity, modesty, honesty, and simplicity. It did not hurt that his customers were blind to the rapacity of his mind or the mendacity in his soul.

He learned some hard lessons early on. He learned to avoid assumptions. He learned not to ambush. He told me his first job was as a vacuum-cleaner salesman and he wanted to make a fast impression and to overwhelm. When a lady opened her door, he rushed past her and dropped a pile of cow shit on her Persian carpet and said, "This vacuum is a technological marvel and if it does not clean every inch of that mess, I'll eat it!" She said, "Would you prefer ketchup or mustard?" He said, "Pardon?" She said, "We just arrived. There's no electricity."

Chas found that the best way to close a sale after pretending to befriend a homeowner was to miss a four-inch putt.

Chas came up the drive of a promising luxury home and asked a little girl sitting near the door and playing with her dolls if her father was home. She nodded in the affirmative. He rang the bell over and over but no one came to the door. Exasperated, he asked the child, "Why did you say he was home?" She said, "He is. I live over there."

For a long time, when Chas was selling alarm systems, his sales were below average and the product manager at the factory suggested he might not be positive enough. He suggested, "Maybe you should focus on a positive word and use it all the time." Chas tried it and sales went up. If a customer talked about her husband's new job, he said, "That's wonderful!" If another bragged about his kid, he said, "How wonderful!" If another raved about her new hairdo, he said, "It's wonderful." I asked him what he used to say before he discovered his "positive" word, and he said, "I could give a shit!"

Chas rang the bell of an apartment in an upscale high-rise. A teenage girl answered the door smoking a cigarette and holding a beer while her friends boogied to loud rap music behind her. He shouted, "Is your mother home?" She took a puff and said, "You're kidding, right?"

For a brief period, Chas was selling burial plots to the aged and infirm. He was starting his pitch to one rickety customer, when the guy said, "I'm sorry but we have burial plots in another cemetery." 'Oh," Chas hesitated, "Well, I hope you'll be very happy there."

Freddie

CAN YOU IMAGINE HOW EMBARRASSING it must be? Can you imagine failing time after time? Can you imagine having to apologize again and again? It would be enough to drive a man to drink. It would be enough to drive him insane. It would be enough to drive him to celibacy. It would be enough to drive him to suicide. Freddie had all these thoughts and emotions pass through his suffering brain because he was the leading premature ejaculator in the United States, or at least he thought he was. If being gay would solve his problem, he would become one with alacrity. If castration would ease his pain, he would slice and dice without hesitation. He wished, he prayed, he longed for a mutual orgasm. And he was furious the powers that be put him in this position.

He was reading in his girlfriend Loretta's living room one day while she was cooking in the kitchen and she asked him to come help her. She was in panties and bra when he arrived and she threw herself at him with abandon, pushed him to the floor, and straddled him, pulling her panties to the side. As always, he was both elated and terrified. He prayed for staying power but after a short time, he came, and she immediately hopped off and casually resumed cooking. He asked, "What was the purpose of that?" She answered, "I broke the egg timer."

He concluded with sorrow that premature ejaculation was nature's cruelest compliment.

On occasion, he could laugh at himself. We went to dinner one night and he said he read an article where researchers concluded premature ejaculation was genetic. He said, "I think it's true. I was with Loretta and prematurely ejaculated in my 'genes' an hour ago." I laughed so he continued, "While we were fooling around, I dialed the premature ejaculation hotline for help and got as far as: 212-965-6…"

After suffering for years, Freddie sought medical assistance. The doctor examined him and said, "Unfortunately, I can't cure you, but I do know a woman with a short attention span."

Freddie had a friend Carl who tried to stop his own premature ejaculation by startling himself at the crucial moment. It was a procedure recommended by his sex therapist. He bought a gun and fired it just as he was about to come in the "69" position with his wife. Freddie asked, "Did it work?" Carl answered, "God, no. My wife bit my cock, peed on my chin, and the gardener jumped out of the closet with his hands up."

In desperation, Freddie went to a sex shop and bought a can of Ever Hard spray. The clerk said it would make him last for hours. It did not work. He came faster than ever. He went back to the sex shop, slammed the can on the counter, and said, "This was useless!" The clerk examined the can and asked, "Did you keep the Ever Hard on your work bench?" Freddie said, "Yeah, so what." The clerk said, "This is turpentine."

Miriam

MIRIAM BECAME A BIBLE SALESWOMAN because she failed at being a Jehovah's Witness. Although she loved Christ deeply, she could not bring herself to believe that he was God's only creation, and that everything else was created through him. She could not believe that God would surrender his power to create a perfect universe in that way. Besides, evangelism made her itch and Armageddon made her hiccup. When she found out 100 million bibles are printed every year and annual sales exceed $425 million, she wanted in on the action. It made no difference to her if the sales were door-to-door, by mail, through bookstores, or via gift shops. She came at you like the gay, 50-year-old whirling dervish she was, but with a twinkle in her eye.

For a while Miriam sold bibles in freezing Minnesota. She became friendly with a local priest who visited her apartment one afternoon. He asked her how she was handling the cold? She said, "Father, if it were not for my scotch and soda and my rosary, I think I'd never get warm. By the way, would you like a drink?" He said, "That would ne nice." She yelled toward the kitchen, "Rosary, please bring Father Hanley a scotch and soda!"

One of her best gigs was when she was selling bibles on a cruise ship. As she relaxed on deck, a very agitated man ran by and yelled, "Is there a priest on board?" When no one answered, he yelled, "Is there a minister on board?" When no one answered, he yelled, "Is there a rabbi on board?" He was so distraught when no one answered that Miriam went up to him and said, "I sell bibles. Can I help?" He said, "Shit, no. I need a corkscrew!"

I met Miriam when she was selling bibles in England. We had a drink and a friend of hers joined us. He sold bibles, too, and was rather annoyed but philosophical about something that had just happened to him. Miriam asked, "What was it?" He said, "My wife and I wanted to join a local church. The vicar said we had to avoid sex for a fortnight to prove our devotion. We almost made it but I saw her bending over and I simply couldn't resist. The vicar banned us from the parish." Miriam asked, "Is that a problem for you?" He responded, "I guess not. We're banned from Harrods, too."

Miriam was doing so well selling bibles, she decided to hire a second salesman to increase her profits and interviewed several for the job. On a trial basis, she hired a man who stuttered and gave him 30 bibles to sell as a test, and he sold them all in one day. Then, he sold 50 in one day. Then, he sold 80 in one day. She was amazed and asked how he did it. He said, "I s-say t-to c-c-c-customers, w-w-would y-you l-l-like to b-b-buy a b-b-bible or w-w-would you p-p-prefer I r-r-read it t-to you?"

Miriam asked me, "Can you tell me what happened when a priest, a minister and a rabbi went into the jungle with their holy books, returned without them, and the rabbi was badly mauled?" I said, "No, what." She said, "It's obvious. The priest gave a gorilla Holy Communion, the minister baptized him, and the rabbi tried to circumcise him."

Qu'in

Qu'in, China's foremost historian, does not have a specialty, or a sub-specialty, or even a sub-sub-specialty. His focus is strictly on The Silk Road. Thus, he pays very little attention to the Shang Dynasty, which asserted control over much of the Yellow River Valley, or the Zhou Dynasty which expanded the kingdom into the Yangtze River Valley, or the Qin Dynasty, which was responsible for The Great Wall and the Terra Cotta Soldiers. No, he focuses exclusively on The Silk Road established during the Han Dynasty: a network of footpaths and caravan trails across rugged mountains and barren deserts linking China to the Mediterranean from the second century B.C.E. to the seventh century C.E. Since Qu'in looks like Charlie Chan, and wears coke-bottle glasses, his brilliance is disguised until he speaks, and his wit until he winks.

When he was a very young scholar, Qu'in was studying some ancient texts along The Silk Road in Samarkand. They told of a prostitute who was a victim of Chinese duplicity, even then. She took a young Chinese traveler to her bed. He was most vigorous, and asked to rest afterward in her slumber yurt. After recovering, he came back in and was more energetic than before. He rested again, came back again, and was even more spirited. This happened six times until she was exhausted. Needing rest herself, she went to her slumber yurt, pulled the curtain aside, and discovered six Chinese.

I was an archeology student for a short time and was lucky enough to join Qi'in on a dig near Xian where a mass grave was discovered containing 5,000 massacred Chinese soldiers. Over dinner he said to me, "Do you know the worst thing about massacring 5,000 Chinese soldiers?" I said, "I have no idea." He said with his mouth full, "An hour later, you want to do it again."

Qu'in attended a conference of Asian scholars in Shanghai discussing newly found camel routes near Bagdad on The Silk Road. There were so many languages being spoken, everyone agreed to speak English, including an elderly Japanese academic who had not fully mastered the language. Qu'in was with him when he went to exchange some money at the hotel front desk and was only given 600 Yuan for 1,000 Yen. He complained that five days ago he received 700 Yuan for 1,000 Yen. The clerk said, "Fluctuations," and the academic shot back, "Fluck you too, Plick!"

Qu'in's travels took him to Tyre, Lebanon, and he used the opportunity to cross the border into Israel to visit the Hebrew University of Jerusalem. He told me about a conversation he had with a professor there who had discovered some new Dead Sea Scrolls. Qu'in related, "The professor told me he found a parable in one of the scrolls in which Jesus joined three men traveling in a cart to Bethlehem. They all had terrible afflictions and Jesus could see they required the love and mercy of his ministry. One had leprosy and Jesus touched his shoulder and he was healed. Another lost his hearing and Jesus touched his ear and he could hear. As Jesus turned to the third man, he lurched away and cried, 'Not me! Not me! I'm on disability pension!'

Part 10

Josh

WHEN HE FIRST STARTED PRACTICING psychiatry, Josh adopted Adler's approach of individual psychology, then Freud's approach of psychoanalysis, and then Jung's approach of analytical psychology. He never regretted joining a medical specialty devoted to the diagnosis, prevention, study, and treatment of mental disorders, whether relating to mood, behavior, cognition or perception. Currently, he employs the combined treatment of psychiatric medication and psychotherapy, and sees clients on both an in-patient and outpatient basis. He is so attractive, kind and understanding at 43 that "transference," the redirection of a patient's feelings from one person to the therapist, is often a problem. Though he never breaches patient confidentiality, he does like to tell humorous stories out of school, but only on an anonymous basis.

Early in his career, a patient came to see Josh and told him he was obsessed with sex and it was ruining his life. Josh showed the patient a photo of a man and woman making love and asked him what he saw and he said correctly, "They're having sex." The trouble was he gave the very same answer to photos of two loco-motives colliding, the Verrazano Bridge, a bottle of milk, and snow in the woods. Josh observed, "You do appear to be preoccupied with sex," and the patient snorted, "Me? You're the one with the filthy pictures!"

I referred a case to Josh where the patient claimed to have an un-controllable urge to insert his member into a blender at the veg-etable canning factory where he worked. Josh thought long and hard about it and consented to it because, if done with medical precision, it might have a more therapeutic effect on the patient than letting him obsess about it for the rest of his life. I asked how it turned out. He said, "Not so hot. When the patient inserted his member into the blender, they were both terminated."

When a patient told Josh he had suicidal inclinations and could kill himself at any time, Josh made him pay in advance.

Josh had to institutionalize an eminent physicist for years and con-tinued seeing him on an inpatient basis. Because the man appeared to be making great progress, Josh considered releasing him and asked him what he would do if he got out. He said, "I might go back to conducting high-frequency particle accelerator tests, but without stress, or writing a book on time moving in opposite direc-tions in the same universe, but without deadlines." Josh was very encouraged. The physicist continued, "And if none of those things work out, I can always be a coffee pot again."

To streamline his practice, Josh decided to make use of a prere-corded phone message. It said, "If you have a multiple-personality disorder, push "GHI" and "TUV." If you are a manic-depressive, no one cares which button you push. If you are an obsessive-compulsive, push "DEF" again and again. If you are schizophrenic, a sprite will tell you what to push. If you are co-dependent, ask someone nearby to push "JKL" for you."

Buddy

IT IS HARD TO GET a cab in New York. It is even harder to get a medallion. Canary Yellow Medallion taxicabs are generally concentrated in the borough of Manhattan, but patrol throughout the five boroughs of the city and may be hailed with a raised hand or a whistle or by standing at a taxi stand. The medallions are sold by either the city or a prior owner. They cost about $2,500 dollars in 1947 and about $690,000 dollars today. Buddy does not own his own cab; he leases it from an investment company. He is talkative in his taxi and a hail-fellow-well-met in bars. He has been driving cabs for 30 years, loves the moniker "hack," and has yet to meet a fare he cannot tickle.

Buddy picked up a woman on 54th Street who wanted to go to Penn Station. Before she got in the cab, she pulled off her coat, tossed it aside, and jumped in stark naked. She looked at Buddy with contempt, and said, "What are you looking at?" He said, "I don't see how you're gonna pay the fare." She put her heels on the back of the front seat, spread her legs, exposed her heavenly chamber, and said, "How about with this?" Buddy said, "You got anything smaller?"

I was riding shotgun in Buddy's cab one night when he stopped at Madison Square Garden to pick up a drunk swaying at the curb. The drunk got in and said, "I wanna go to Madison Square Garden." Buddy turned to him, pointed out the window and said, "There's Madison Square Garden." The drunk pulled out a ten, handed it to Buddy, and said, "Next time don't drive so fucking fast!"

Buddy told me he likes to play a game on unwitting passengers should they tap him on the shoulder to ask a question. He pretends to swerve and lose control of the cab and screams "Don't do that!" The passenger invariably asks, "Why would a light tap on the shoulder bother you so much?" He answers, "This is my first day in cabs. I drove a hearse for ten years."

Occasionally, a cab driver gets an opportunity to take revenge on a detestable passenger. One passenger on Buddy's regular patrol route, whom he did not like, kept bringing hookers into his cab. Buddy noticed his first name was Arthur from his credit card. One day, Arthur got into the cab with what must have been his wife because she was lambasting him about his infidelity. He denied it vociferously. Buddy turned around and said to him, "Gee, Art, you got a real bitch to fuck this time!"

Buddy carried some important passengers in his day but none more important than the Pope. When the Pope's plane landed in New York, there was a snafu with his luggage so he hopped in Buddy's cab to rush to the city. Traffic was so bad the Pope asked Buddy if he could drive, so Buddy hopped in the back. A cop stopped them for speeding but hesitated giving them a ticket until he talked to his captain. He called in and said, "I'm not sure I should give this ticket. There's someone very important in the cab." The captain asked, "How can you tell"? The cop answered, "The Pope is his driver."

Martha

You would not know it, but when Martha looked at her toys as a child, she was really only interested in the numbers on them. The same was true for license plates when she got a bit older. And it held true all the way through math games for kids; algebra and calculus in high school; and math and economics in college. Her favorite courses were International Economics and Comparative Economic Systems. She graduated *summa cum laude* with a degree in international money and finance and has worked at the World Bank in Washington as a senior financial risk analyst for the last 15 years. Now, at 36, she is a happily married woman with two kids, a job she loves, and a droll view of the merits of her profession

Before Martha left on an extended trip abroad, she drove her Maserati to a bank near the entrance to Dulles International Airport. She went in to see the loan officer and asked for a $3,000 loan during a low-interest promotion. He agreed and, per bank policy, put her car in the bank's garage as collateral until she returned in three months. When she arrived back in town, she went to the bank and repaid the $3,000 plus $180 in interest. The banker said, "You're obviously wealthy. Why would you need a $3,000 loan?" She said, "Let's see you park a car at Dulles for three months for only $180."

I interviewed Martha when I was writing an article on World Bank loan programs. She was depressed by all the poverty in the world and told me the sad story of a man in The Gambia whom she visited in his hut. He told her, "When I had to sell house, I ask God to win lottery. Nothing. I ask same thing before selling jalopy, cattle, and daughter. Nothing. Now, you be witness. I ask God to win lottery so don't have to sell wife." Just then a shaft of light pierced the roof of the hut, and God said to him, "Come on, Akono, help me out here. Buy a ticket."

Martha told me, "Noah was the greatest economist who ever lived because he floated a new enterprise while the whole world was in liquidation, and that only an economist could find something that works perfectly in practice but not in theory."

She opened a speech with this story at The World Economic Forum in Davos: "A mathematician, an accountant and an economist interview for the same job. They enter the interview room one after the other. Each is asked, 'What does four times four equal?' The mathematician says, 'Eight, precisely.' The accountant says, 'Eight, on average, give or take 5%.' The economist looks around to see if anyone is listening, and whispers to the interviewer, 'What would you like it to equal?'"

Martha asked, "Did you know economists predicted ten out of last the six recessions?"

She also joined some other economists climbing a mountain in Switzerland and they got hopelessly lost. One examined his map, looked around carefully, and said, "See that mountain to the south? Well, according to my calculations, we're standing on top of it!"

Juan

BULLFIGHTS HAVE EXISTED IN ONE form or another since 2000 B.C.E. They were a popular spectacle in ancient Rome but it was in the Iberian Peninsula that the contests were fully developed. The Moors, mounted on horses, observed feast days by killing bulls in a ritualistic fashion. The modern *corrida* began to take shape when men on foot aided horsemen with their cape work, and from 1726 to today the spectacle has remained the same with the addition of the *estoque* (sword) and *muleta* (small, worsted cape). Juan is the leader of an entourage and the one who kills the bull. He is called *matador*. The others who fight the bull in the ring are called *toreros*. Juan is a pompous ass.

Juan invested in a restaurant called *The Picador*. An American came in after a *corrida* and noticed a customer eating spaghetti with two huge meatballs. He was told they were bull's testicles. He ordered the dish but they were out for the day. The same thing happened the next day, and the next. Finally, he showed up at opening time on the day after some novices were allowed to train in the bullring. Juan brought him the dish but it only had two small balls in it. The

American growled, "What the hell is this?" Juan replied, 'I'm sorry, Senor. The bull does not always lose."

Juan told me a friend of his, another matador, met an untimely death. He said, "My friend was still wearing his bullfighting costume when his house caught fire and he was forced to flee to the roof. To show he was fearless, he strutted around and ignored all the firemen's entreaties for him to jump into the safety net until they were thoroughly disgusted with him. Finally, when the flames were too high, he leaped and just as he was about to hit the net the firemen yanked it away and shouted, 'Ole!'"

Juan had a dream where a father and a son bull were standing on a hill in France overlooking a herd of cows. The son said, "Papa, let's run down the hill and screw a couple of cows." The father said languidly, "No son, let's walk down and screw them all."

Juan's dream continued: "The bulls herded the cows into a line and the father started on one end and the son on the other. The father said slowly, 'Bonjour.... Merci....Bonjour....Merci.' The son said quickly, 'Bonjour, Merci, Bonjour, Merci.' The father said, 'Bonjour... Merci...Bonjour...Merci.' The son said, "Bonjour, Merci, Bonjour Merci, Pardon, Papa! Bonjour, Merci…"

Juan was strolling through the barn at a bull auction with a girlfriend who had become a harridan over time. He wanted to get rid of her but no matter what he said, she brushed it aside. He was wondering if there was any insult that would faze her. She was admiring the bulls and reading the signs on their stalls. One said, "This bull mated 40 times last year!" and she said "Oooh!" The next sign said, "This bull mated 80 times last year!" and she gasped, "Oh, my!"

The next sign said, "This bull mated 130 times last year!" and she turned to Juan and said, "Why can't you be like that?" He turned to her and snarled, "I doubt if it was with the same tired cow!"

Dirk

Dirk has been a coal miner for 20 years. He has no formal education and relies on common sense, on-the-job training, and trial and error to master his craft. He works underground with lignite, bituminous and anthracite coal; is athletic and realistic; has great manual dexterity; and can operate complex machinery. As a consequence, he has moved up the ranks over the years from laborer to coal miner to helper to supervisor. He is a member of the United Mine Workers of America and a fierce advocate for higher wages, better working conditions, and improved health care. Dirk is a good neighbor, a loyal friend, a tireless worker, and a closet wise guy.

Dirk was escorting a woman executive from headquarters through his mine's business office. There was a large framed photo on the wall of three naked black men standing in front of the mine's entrance. Two of the men had black penises and the one in the middle had a pink penis. She said, "I'm glad to see we have African Americans working at the mine." Dirk said, "They're not African

Americans. They're white and covered with coal dust and the one in the middle went home for lunch."

Over drinks, Dirk told me that coal mining was dangerous in ways people could not imagine. A local miner's son who had become a famous pianist and composer agreed to perform a concert at the top of the mineshaft to be broadcast throughout the mine. Unfortunately, the movers pushing his piano into position lost control of it and it fell down the shaft crushing a miner to death. It was a tragedy, and the pianist, to honor the miner's memory, wrote a musical tribute entitled, "Concerto In A Flat Miner."

Dirk was giving me a tour of the mine when there was great commotion at the head of the coal seam. The men had stumbled across what appeared to be fossilized plant life 1,200 feet down. Based on his years of experience, Dirk knew this could be a major scientific discovery, so he suspended work in the shaft and called in a botanist. The botanist arrived three days later and examined the plant and told Dirk it looked like a fern that was discovered in the Great Rift Valley in Africa and was used by prehistoric man to fight constipation. Dirk opined, "With fronds like these, who needs enemas."

Dirk's son Bruce, also a jester, attended the local high school and his teacher asked the class, "Can you choose a year and tell me the number of tons of coal produced in the United States that year?" The class was quiet until Bruce pierced the silence with, "1396 and zero."

A miner hit a wall with a pickax unleashing a jet of water that soaked him. He plugged it up, went to the surface, and looked five years younger. His co-miners were astonished, so they too stood in front of the jet and they too looked five years younger when they sur-faced. The first miner mused to Dirk, "Why only five years? Why not ten or 20 or 30?" Dirk thought it was a good question, reflected on it, and said, "I guess it was only intended to be a miner miracle."

Philomena

PHILOMENA IS AN EARLY GREEK name now used in various Latin countries. In Greek myth, Philomena was an Athenian princess who was transformed by the gods into a nightingale to save her from the advances of a lecherous king. That being the case, it stands to reason that the name would be used by our own Philomena: a 36-year-old beautician in Oxnard. She became a licensed beautician after obtaining a high school degree, completing a cosmetology program, and passing a state-mandated exam. One could best sum up her attitude toward her customers by repeating a phrase she once used when a less-than-comely customer left her beauty shop. She said, "Someone must have hit that bitch with an ugly stick!"

Philomena told me what happened when she and a rather dim-witted fellow beautician named Lorna went on a river-rafting trip in the Grand Canyon with two of their friends. The guide cautioned them that it could get very, very, hot so they should bring something to stay cool. One friend brought an ice chest for her drinks. Another brought a hat with a small electric fan on the brim. Philomena brought lightweight mesh clothing. And Lorna brought a car door so she could roll down the window and catch the breeze.

Philomena asked me if I knew how to tell if a woman had a facelift? I said, "No, how?" She said, "When you squeeze her tits, her mouth and eyes pop open."

She also worked with a particular customer for years whom she loved dearly, but who spent way too much time worrying about staying youthful and beautiful. Philomena was afraid she would go too far. One day she came into the salon and confided to Philomena that she had been given a facelift and was using a new device implanted by the plastic surgeon to keep her skin taut. It was a screw in the back of her neck that she could turn to tighten things up. She complained, "I've been turning and turning the screw but I still have bags under my eyes." Philomena whispered to her, "Those aren't bags, they're your tits, and if you turn the screw any more, you're going to have a beard."

I was visiting Philomena's in her salon when a rather stout, red-faced woman in a furious mood swept in, collapsed into a styling chair, and hissed, "That bastard!" Philomena exclaimed, "What's wrong, Flo?" She said, "I asked my husband if he would still love me when I'm old and fat and ugly and he said, 'Of course I do.'"

It happens that Philomena really dislikes vain women and would prefer they take their business elsewhere. So, she insults them. One asked with a look of concern, "I spend so much time in front of the mirror admiring my beauty. Do you think it's vanity?" Philomena replied, "No, imagination." Another mused, "I think I have a face that's timeless." Philomena said, "Yes, it could stop an eight-day clock." A third said haughtily, "I'm going to interview for a job as a television personality." Philomena encouraged her with, "You should. You have the perfect face for radio." And a fourth asked, "Will I lose my looks as I get older?" Philomena answered, "Hopefully, yes."

Armando

THEY ARE CALLED MANY NAMES: *cowboy* in the U.S; *gaucho* in Argentina, Uruguay and southern Brazil; *vaqueiro* in northern Brazil; *huaso* in Chile; and *llanero* in Columbia and Venezuela. Armando's venue is the great wide plains of Argentina, called *pampas*. He is a swarthy, 49-year-old nomad, a colorful horseman and cowhand, and as much a folk hero in Argentina as the cowboy is in North America. His tools are the lasso, the knife, and the *bolas*, a device made of leather cords and three iron balls that is thrown at the legs of an animal to entwine and immobilize it. Deep down, he knows his profession is an anachronism, and worthy of jest, but he just loves it too much to quit.

After coming off the pampas and an afternoon of drinking, Armando and his friends went to a rickety cinema to see a movie in Perito Moreno. They noticed a gaucho sprawled over several seats three rows ahead of them but thought nothing of it, assuming he was as drunk as they were. Apparently, occupying so many seats violated theater policy so he was asked to occupy one seat only by the usher, then the manager, and finally a policeman, but he would not budge.

The policeman, now angry, demanded, "What is your name?" The gaucho slurred, "Santiago." The policeman asked, "Where are you from?" The gaucho mumbled, "The balcony, you idiot."

Armando was my guide on a visit to Patagonia. He rode alongside me and told me a story about a simple gaucho named Javier who, along with two other gauchos, came within a hair of being unjustly hanged for cattle rustling. It was a case of mistaken identity. The noose was placed on a tree overhanging the Deseado River so the desperadoes could be dropped into the river after hanging. The first two gauchos slipped out of the noose from either perspiration or grease, dropped into the river, and swam to freedom. As his captors slipped the noose around Javier's neck, he pleaded with them in desperation, "Tighter...no, tighter...no, tighter...I can't swim!"

Armando boasted about two things: First, he claimed he could look a bull in the eye and tell what it was thinking, and second, he was one of the first gauchos to participate in the collection of sperm from a bull using an artificial vagina. The water in the liner of the vagina was to be set at 42–48 degrees Celsius, but by mistake Armando set it at 62-68 degrees Celsius. The bull mounted the teaser cow, inserted its penis into the sleeve held by Armando, let out a tremendous bellow, and jumped back utterly bewildered. I asked Armando, "What was the bull thinking?" He said, "What a woman!"

Armando also likes to tell a story about a worthy gaucho who appears before St. Peter at the Pearly Gates and seeks admittance. St. Peter asks, "Have you done any good deeds to justify your entry into heaven?" The gaucho replies, "Yes, I rode into Valcheto to eat at the cantina and saw a gang of outlaws molesting a lovely seno-rita. I beat the hell out of the leader and threatened to take on the rest of the gang. They surrounded me with bolas and knives." St. Peter said, "And how long ago did this occur?" The gaucho said, "About five minutes ago."

Rosemary

WHEN SHE WROTE HER PROFILE for the online dating site, Rosemary followed these simple rules: Be exciting; be creative; the fewer "I's" the better; use proper spelling and grammar; leave sex out of it; do not brag; do not make demands; be true to yourself; and end with a hook. She was aware of the pitfalls: free sites imply no commitment and paid sites imply desperation; online dating limits connections; selections become predictable; personality tests are flawed; there are too many magic angles on photos and posts from the past; and more relationships begin from blogs or Twitter than dating sites. She did not care. She was beautiful, smart, 24, and in it for the laughs.

Most of the men Rosemary dated said they loved babies to enhance their credibility. One even asked to meet her in the park and he arrived pushing a baby carriage with a screaming infant in it. He said soothingly, "It's all right, Bill," and "Don't cry, Bill" and "Stay calm, Bill." She said of the baby, "Bill's a real handful, huh?" He said, "I'm Bill."

Rosemary hooked up "for coffee only" with a really annoying guy who grilled her on her attitude toward children. To test her suitability, he asked, "Suppose my parents showed up at an inconvenient time and asked to see the baby. What would you say?" "I would say, "Soon."" "What if they asked again in half an hour?" "I would say, 'Not just yet.'" "What if they insisted after an hour?" "I would say, 'Wait until it cries.'" "Why would you say that?" "Because I forgot where I dropped it."

To impress her, one date took her to the finest restaurant in the city and she decided to go all out: cocktail, escargots, salad nicoise, fine wine, filet mignon, assorted cheeses, cherries jubilee, café latte and port. His patience at an end, he asked angrily, "Does your father allow you to eat at home like this?" She replied, "I would say no, but he's also not trying to get laid."

On another occasion at a fine restaurant, her date, wanting to appear the gourmet, asked her if she would like to try bird's nest soup. She said, "I've never had it before. Is it really a nest?" He said, "Yes, it's held together with the bird's saliva." She said, "Yuck!" I'm not going to eat spit that came out of a bird's mouth." He said, "Well, what would you like?" She said, "Eggs benedict."

She said of a disappointing lover she met online, "He has delusions of adequacy."

Rosemary told me she accepted an offer from a promising online date to spend a weekend at a luxury hotel. I asked, "Did it turn out well?" She said, "No, it was terrible. I had to say something offensive to get him to cut it short." I asked, "What did you say?" She said, "Well, he was a real show off. He did a one-and-a-half gainer into the pool and bragged he was on his college diving team. So I jumped into the pool and did 15 laps in record time. He asked me, 'Did you swim in college?' I answered, 'No, I was a prostitute in Panama City and worked both sides of the canal.'"

Mutengke

MUTENGKE IS A MEMBER OF the Korowai Tribe in Western New Guinea. The Korowai are one of the few tribes believed to eat human flesh as a cultural practice. If it involves consumption of a person within the same community, it is called *endocannibalism* and can be part of the grieving process or a way of guiding the souls of the dead into bodies of living descendants. If it is the consumption of a person from outside the community, it is called *exocannibalism* and is usually related to the celebration of victory over an enemy. In either case, it is believed eating a person endows the cannibal with some of the characteristics of the deceased. When Mutengke is in the mountains, he is a cannibal. When he is in Port Moresby, he is an investment banker.

Mutengke told me a cannibal is a guy who goes into a restaurant and orders the waiter. He also said that when two cannibals are eating soup and one says, "I hate my brother," the other says, "Just eat the croutons."

Mutengke's tribe captured three scientists on an expedition in the mountains. One was Japanese, one was English, and one was

American. The Chief told them they would be killed, eaten, and their skins would be used for canoes. He gave them the option of suicide. The Japanese took out his machete, yelled, "Banzai!" and plunged it into his abdomen. The Englishman raised his gourd, shouted, "To King And Country!" and shot himself through the heart. The American hollered, "Give Me Liberty or Give Me Death!" and punctured himself all over his body with his fork. As he bled out, the Chief asked, "Why you do that?" He snorted, "Try paddling *this* canoe, you son-of-a-bitch!"

I asked Mutengke when was the last time he engaged in cannibalism. He said, "About a year ago a minister from Bougainville who was thought to be a very good man came into the mountains to heal the sick and convert the heathen. He was only in our village three days when he was captured, killed, cooked and eaten. Within hours everyone in the village was sick as a dog. The tribe sent me to the witch doctor to ask why were we all throwing up so much. He told me, 'Everyone know. Can't keep good man down.'"

That was the incident that ended Mutengke's cannibalism for good. But you might say he was prepped for it by the very same witch doctor whom he visited after killing and broiling a fat, bald, white man who wore sandals and a robe held shut by a hemp rope. After eating the man, Mutengke became ill. He went to the witch doctor and in local patois said, "How come I sick?" The witch doctor replied, "That not broiler. That friar."

The Korowai conduct elaborate ceremonies before killing and eating their victims. A silver throne is stored in the attic of the chief's grass house and is brought down so he can view the proceedings in royal comfort. Unfortunately, after a night of wild dancing, the floor of the attic collapsed and the falling throne killed the chief. Mutengke asked the witch doctor if it was a bad omen, and he said ruefully, "People who live in grass houses shouldn't stow thrones."

Consuela

CONSUELA'S NAME IS DERIVED FROM a Latin word meaning "consolation." She consoled her parents when her brother died at home in Matamoros. She consoled her boyfriend before he was sent to prison for 40 years. She consoled her aunt as she died from cancer. She consoled the frightened Guatemalan family as a *Coyotaje* led them across the Mexican-U.S. border. And once in the U.S., as a maid, she consoled her wounded employers: the hysterical socialite whose husband left her; the lawyer on drugs who lost his license; and the elderly woman who lost her dog. Finally, at 26, she found stability as a chambermaid in a five-star hotel. Though short, stout, nearsighted, and hard of hearing, she was nevertheless ready to begin her quixotic quest for a *gringo* husband.

When Consuela first started at the hotel, she had to work the night shift. She therefore left work in the wee hours. As she passed a bar on the way to the bus stop, she noticed two things: the patrons in the bar were drunk and howling loud and there was a police car hiding nearby to catch drunk drivers. She moved on and while she was waiting at the bus stop the police car pulled a drunk driver over right in front of her. The cops gave the driver a Breathalyzer test but it was negative. They thought their equipment was broken. The driver said, "I don't think so. I'm the designated decoy."

Consuela was told by management to be very quiet and respectful cleaning Room 504, which was occupied by a grieving widow who had checked in early after her husband's funeral. As she made the bed, she stole glances at the desolate widow who was sitting by the window watching the rain. The widow sighed and said to no one in particular, "You can spend your whole life helping others and being adored, but when all is said and done, the size of the crowd at your funeral depends on the weather."

On another occasion, Consuela knocked on the door of Suite 810 and when no one answered went in to clean and startled a young man snorting a line of coke on a table covered with cash. He said sheepishly, "I'm sorry, Miss, but as you can see, cocaine is God's way of saying you're making too much money."

I attended a lecture at Consuela's hotel on female hormones. She was there to help clean up the hall but arrived early, stood at the back, and listened to the speaker's conclusion. I asked her if she learned anything and she said, "Si, Senor. I learn the way women like men depend on menstrual cycle. If she in middle, she like handsome, strong man. If she have period, she like man with knife in head, gag in mouth, who on fire."

Consuela was cleaning the bathroom in Room 2203 when an earthquake hit the hotel and she rushed into the bedroom to get under the bed. The occupants, a husband and wife who had returned early without her knowing it, were having a tremendous argument. The wife pulled off her top and roared, "If I have to die, is there anyone in this room that can make me feel like a woman?" The husband threw off his jacket, ripped off his shirt, handed it to her, and said, "Here, iron this."

Made in United States
North Haven, CT
21 January 2022

15073479R00186